Inside *the* System, Outside *the* Power
Women, Technology, and the Future of AI

Tadia Rice, CISS

ISBN 979-8-9948025-6-4

Published by Blue Horizon Press

Author contact: https://www.tadiarice.com

Printed in the United States of America

DEDICATION

To my daughter and her daughters

and their daughters.

For the women who carried the system

without being allowed to shape it.

For the intelligence that was present

even when it was not credited.

For the care that sustained

what power would not name.

You repaired what you did not break.

You saw the flaw before it scaled.

You were not mistaken.

You were positioned.

All that you touch, you change.

All that you change, changes you.

The only lasting truth is change.

Octavia E. Butler

INTRODUCTION

This book is not an argument against technology.

It is an argument against paternalism, and against the quiet compliance it trained women to mistake for survival.

For generations, women were taught to navigate systems designed without them by becoming agreeable, useful, and indispensable, but never authoritative. Their intelligence was welcomed when it stabilized institutions, absorbed consequence, or softened failure. It was dismissed when it questioned design, challenged power, or refused deference.

This was not accidental.
It was how paternalism preserved itself.

Paternalism does not look like hostility. It looks like guidance. Protection. Expertise. It tells women they are valued, as long as they do not insist on authorship. It rewards adaptation while penalizing refusal. And it teaches women to doubt themselves rather than the structures that constrain them.

This book names that pattern because it is time to end it. Women did not leave technology.

They were redirected into roles that preserved continuity without granting control. What was framed as emotional labor was often advanced situational intelligence — anticipatory, contextual, and exercised without institutional power. Women learned to see what systems would break, who would pay the cost, and how harm would compound, and were told this knowledge was peripheral. It was not.

As artificial intelligence reshapes how decisions are made and justified, the old bargains are no longer viable. Systems that separate authority from responsibility fail. Systems that mistake speed for competence collapse. Systems that continue to treat women's intelligence as optional will not endure.

This book examines how that separation became structural, how it shaped authority in technological institutions, and why intelligent systems now make its consequences visible.

This book is written for women who are done translating themselves into acceptability.

For women who are finished waiting to be invited into rooms built with their labor.

For women who no longer accept the lie that completion requires approval, partnership, or permission.

The future will not be shaped by the most optimized minds, but by the most grounded ones. Parenting, in this sense, is not separate from governance. It is its earliest form.

You do not need to become harder.
You need to become unavailable to distortion.

This is not a request for inclusion. It is a reckoning with design.
Anger, when it arises, is often recognition. Clarity is the beginning of authorship.
It is not over.

And you are not here to be finished by anyone else.

Many women reading this book are not only navigating institutions. They are raising a new generation that will have to operate within them. In an age of artificial intelligence, this matters. The question is no longer how to prepare children to compete with machines, but how to raise humans who can govern power without becoming captive to it. That means teaching sons that authority is not entitlement, and daughters that intelligence does not require permission. It means modeling accountability, emotional regulation, and responsibility for consequence, not dominance, performance, or control.

DECLARATION

This book makes a structural claim.

Authority, as it has been designed in modern technological institutions, has been separated from consequence.

Those who decide are insulated from impact.
Those who absorb impact are excluded from authorship.

This separation is not incidental. It is architectural.

It formed gradually, through redefinition. What counted as technical expertise narrowed. What qualified as leadership consolidated. Intelligence grounded in context, continuity, and downstream consequence was repositioned as support rather than strategy. Responsibility flowed downward. Authority concentrated upstream

Over time, this misalignment appeared normal.

It shaped credibility.
It shaped promotion.
It shaped who was invited to design and who was asked to repair.

The central pattern traced throughout this book is the Authority–Consequence Misalignment Pattern: the structural condition in which decision-making power is insulated from the impact it produces.

When authority and consequence separate, intelligence fragments. Accountability diffuses. Legitimacy erodes.

For decades, this pattern was absorbed quietly within institutions. Women were positioned closest to consequence, asked to stabilize systems they did not author, to translate harm they did not design, and to repair trust without the authority to alter structure.

This arrangement was treated as competence. It was containment.

Artificial intelligence now exposes what was previously absorbed.
Systems that learn, automate, and scale cannot remain governable if authority and consequence remain disconnected. Design decisions propagate widely. Feedback delays become costly. What once accumulated at the margins now accelerates at the center.

The issue is no longer inclusion. It is alignment.

Intelligent systems cannot endure if authority remains distant from impact. Governance cannot remain external to design. Responsibility cannot continue flowing downward while power consolidates upstream.

This book proceeds from that truth.

It argues that durable systems require authorship aligned with consequence. That intelligence must be granted authority where its insights are exercised. That stewardship is not a restraint on innovation but the condition for its survival.

What has been dismissed as emotional, cautious, or peripheral has often been diagnostic.

What has been framed as neutrality has often been insulation.

What has been called resilience has often been exhaustion.

This is not arequest for accommodation.
It is a statement of reality.

Authority must sit closer to consequence.
Responsibility must travel upward with power.
Intelligence must be permitted to shape what it already sustains.

Anything less will not endure.

TABLE OF CONTENTS

CHAPTER 1

Women Did Not Leave Technology

The idea that women "left" technology is one of the most successful mis-directions in modern institutional history. It reframed a structural reallocation of authority as personal choice, allowing systems to preserve power while appearing neutral.

Women didn't leave technology.

They were redirected away,

away from authority,

away from opportunity,

away from authorship,

away from ownership.

They were inside the system, but they were outside the power.

Their intelligence operated within structures that denied them authorship. Their labor sustained systems that excluded them from design.

The definition of technology, what counted as technical, what warranted authority, was redrawn around them. As systems became more valuable, authorship became more restricted. Their intelligence remained. Their names did not.

What changed was not women's participation, but where their intelligence was allowed to operate. As technological systems scaled and decisions accelerated, women were redirected into roles that absorbed consequence without granting authorship, maintaining continuity, mediating failure, and repairing trust while design authority consolidated elsewhere. Their intelligence remained present and operational, but it was no longer recognized as intelligence.

This book begins by correcting that distortion.
That correction requires looking not at who was absent, but at how authority was organized. As computing moved from a marginal discipline into the core infrastructure of institutions, the definition of technical work narrowed even as the systems themselves grew more complex. Tasks associated with consequence, context, and human impact were recategorized

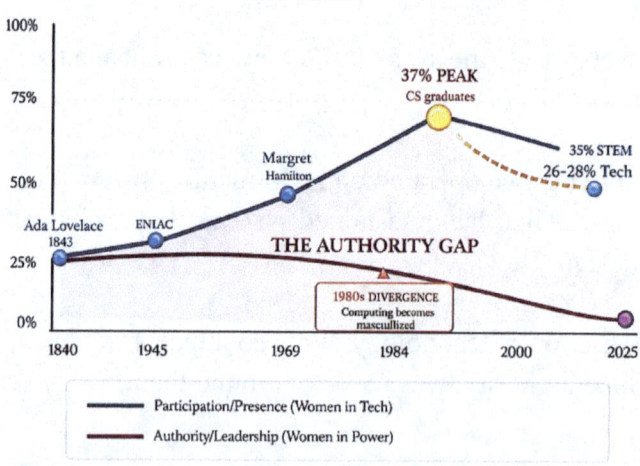

Displacement, Not Departure
Women's Participation vs Authority in Technology
1840–2025

as peripheral instead of technical, while design authority consolidated around abstraction, speed, and scale.

This division did not remove women from technology; it repositioned their intelligence outside the frame of what counted as expertise. The result was a system that continued to rely on women's judgment while erasing their authorship, an arrangement that appeared efficient, but quietly accumulated risk.

This shift was not marked by a single decision or policy. It happened through redefinition. As systems grew more abstract, work that required proximity to users, anticipation of failure, and translation between technical outputs and human consequence was labeled "support," "operations," or "process" — necessary, but not authoritative.

Design was framed as upstream and strategic; consequence was treated as downstream and reactive. Women were overrepresented in the latter not because of preference, but because these roles demanded relational intelligence and accountability without conferring control. What looked like specialization was, in practice, a narrowing of who was allowed to shape the system itself.

This pattern has precedent.

Computing's earliest programmers were women. Ada Lovelace wrote the first algorithm in 1843, recognizing that Charles Babbage's Analytical Engine could process symbols beyond pure calculation.

The six women who programmed ENIAC in 1945 were Betty Jean Jennings, Kay McNulty, Marlyn Wescoff, Ruth Lichterman, Frances Bilas, and Betty Snyder.

They debugged the first general-purpose electronic computer, a system with 18,000 vacuum tubes and five million hand-soldered connections. They developed subroutines, nested loops, and the foundational logic of modern programming without manuals, predecessors, or recognition.

Margaret Hamilton led the software engineering team that put humans on the moon in 1969. She coined the term "software engineering" to legitimize work that was being dismissed as clerical.

Grace Hopper invented the first compiler and developed COBOL, making programming languages comprehensible to humans rather than machines alone.

These women were not assistants to male genius. They were the architects.

Yet by the 1980s, as computing became culturally masculinized and economically valuable, women's presence declined from 37% of computer science graduates in 1984 to 21.3% today. This was not natural attrition. It was structural reallocation masked as preference.

The narrative that women "left" technology became plausible only after their foundational contributions were erased from collective memory.

What drove that reallocation, the structural choices that made it appear inevitable, is examined in the chapter that follows.

What changed was not women's capacity. What changed was who was allowed to claim authorship once the work became prestigious.

How the Redefinition Became Normalized

Once technical authority narrowed, the story that explained it followed. As abstraction, scale, and speed became the dominant measures of technical excellence, proximity to consequence was reframed as distraction rather than intelligence. Work that required sustained attention to users, social context, and long-term impact was recast as secondary, important, but not decisive.

Over time, this distinction hardened into common sense.

Institutional language reinforced the divide. "Hard" skills were associated with design, architecture, and optimization; "soft" skills with communication, coordination, and care.

What was rarely acknowledged was that the latter were not ancillary to system performance; they were compensatory.

They emerged to address what abstraction could not see. As women became concentrated in these roles, the misclassification became self-reinforcing: intelligence expressed relationally was no longer recognized as intelligence at all.

This normalization did not require malice. It required repetition. Hiring criteria, promotion pathways, and prestige markers quietly converged around a narrow definition of technical merit, while the labor that kept systems coherent remained undervalued and under-credited.

Over time, the absence of women from visible authority was taken as evidence of choice or aptitude, rather than as the predictable outcome of design.

The pattern is clear: women did not abandon technology; they were systematically redirected away from its centers of authority.

By 2025, women comprise approximately 26–28% of the global tech workforce, despite representing 42% of the overall labor force.

Women make up 35% of STEM employees in the U.S. yet hold only 21.3% of computer science degrees and 22% of engineering degrees — a decline from 37% in 1985. The direction is not ambiguous.

At the five largest U.S. tech companies, women make up between a third and nearly half of the total workforce. But presence and power are not the same thing.

Presence Is Not the Same as Power

Company	Workforce	Leadership	Gap
Amazon	45%	29%	−16 pts
Meta	36.7%	29%	− 7.7 pts
Apple	35%	31%	−4.0 pts
Google	32.8%	26.7%	−6.1 pts
Microsoft	29%	31.6%	+2.6 pts

Source: WomenTech Network, 2026 Assessment

At four of the five largest tech companies, women's share of leadership is lower than their share of the workforce, and the gap widens at every rung. It compounds in promotion as well: for every 100 men advanced to manager, only 87 women receive the same advancement. For women of color, that number drops to 82.

This is not attrition through choice. It is displacement by design.

The Pattern Repeats in the Age of AI

Artificial intelligence makes this history newly visible.

As decision-making becomes automated and systems act at scale, the same division reappears. Technical authority concentrates around model design, optimization, and deployment, while responsibility for downstream impact, bias, misuse, harm, and loss of trust, is distributed elsewhere.

Ethics reviews, impact assessments, and remediation processes are treated as add-ons rather than as core components of intelligence itself.

Once again, intelligence that anticipates consequence is framed as peripheral.

Once again, those closest to impact are asked to respond after systems are built rather than to shape them before deployment. And once again, women are disproportionately positioned in roles that translate system behavior into human terms, explaining, mitigating, and repairing outcomes they did not design.

The risk is no longer theoretical. Intelligent systems do not fail only through malfunction; they fail through misalignment.

When authority is separated from responsibility, systems accelerate beyond their capacity to be governed. What once appeared efficient becomes brittle.

What was dismissed as caution becomes, in retrospect, foresight.

AI does not create this pattern.
It exposes it.

Why This Matters Now

The claim that women "left" technology collapses under this lens. What occurred was not withdrawal but displacement, of intelligence from authority, of care from design, of responsibility from decision-making. The cost of that displacement is no longer borne quietly at the margins. It is now embedded in systems that shape public life, institutional legitimacy, and collective trust.

Correcting this distortion is not about nostalgia or redress. It is about viability. Systems capable of learning, adapting, and acting at scale cannot be safely governed by abstraction alone. They require intelligence that can hold context, consequence, and continuity simultaneously.

This book proceeds from a simple premise: the intelligence that was sidelined is now indispensable.

That premise has both a moral and an economic foundation. Companies in the top quartile for gender diversity are 25% more likely to report above-average profitability. Legitimacy crises, the direct result of systems that exclude those closest to consequence, cost institutions billions in recovery, regulatory exposure, and eroded public trust. The moral case and the business case are not in tension. They converge.

What follows is not an argument for restoring the past, but for redesigning authority so that intelligence, wherever it operates, can shape the systems it is already sustaining.

CHAPTER 2

The Gendered Architecture of Authority

Power rarely announces itself as exclusion. More often, it arrives as structure.

By the time women's presence in technology appeared to decline, the architecture of authority had already shifted beneath the surface. Decisions about who designed systems, who set priorities, and who defined technical excellence were no longer distributed through visible rules.

They were embedded in norms, pipelines, and organizational design.

Authority did not disappear from women's reach all at once. It was reallocated, quietly, incrementally, and through mechanisms that were difficult to contest precisely because they appeared neutral.

This is how gendered systems endure: not through overt prohibition, but through structural inevitability.

Authority Is Designed, Not Assumed

In theory, technology is meritocratic. Code works or it doesn't. Systems scale or they fail. This narrative is seductive because it implies fairness without effort.

In practice, authority is not granted by competence alone. It is produced by institutional design.

Who gets early access to emerging tools.
Who is invited into decision-making rooms.
Whose mistakes are treated as learning versus disqualification.
Whose leadership is framed as vision rather than risk.

These decisions shape careers long before outcomes can be measured. They determine who accumulates credibility, who gains authorship, and who is positioned as a future leader.

Women were not excluded because they lacked skill. They were excluded because the criteria for authority shifted toward traits and pathways historically coded as masculine, assertiveness over discernment, speed over deliberation, disruption over continuity.

None of these values are inherently male. But once institutions reward them selectively, they begin to function as gatekeeping mechanisms.

The WomenTech Network's 2026 assessment exposes this gendered architecture with precision. Only 8-9% of women hold positions like CIO, CTO, or IT manager. None of the 'Big Five' U.S. tech firms, Alphabet, Apple, Meta, Amazon, Microsoft, has ever had a female CEO. Women hold only 24% of Fortune 500 board seats and just 25% of C-level positions overall, with a mere 5% representing women of color. This is not a pipeline problem.

It is an authority problem.

The Myth of Neutral Systems

One of the most persistent myths in technology is that systems are neutral until people introduce bias. This framing is convenient because it externalizes responsibility.

Every system reflects the assumptions of its designers: what matters, what counts, what can be ignored.

When authority structures privilege individual brilliance over collective intelligence, they obscure relational labor.

When they reward novelty without accountability, they discount stewardship. When they elevate abstraction over lived experience, they devalue contextual insight.

These are not accidents. They are design choices.

Women's labor has historically clustered around the domains that these systems undervalue: integration, translation, ethical foresight, long-term impact. As authority narrowed around a different definition of excellence, women were not pushed out of technology, they were pushed out of its center of power.

The No-Win Evaluation Trap

Women in technical roles face a structural contradiction that no amount of individual performance can resolve. Research demonstrates what many women have long understood: competence and likability are inversely correlated for women in ways they are not for men.

When women demonstrate technical authority, they are penalized for lack of warmth. When they demonstrate collaborative skill, they are seen as less competent. The bind is not personal. It is structural. Women cannot simultaneously meet expectations for technical excellence and social acceptability because those expectations were designed to be mutually exclusive.

This is not a communication problem. It is a design problem. AI systems trained on historical performance evaluations, promotion decisions, and peer assessments encode this bind at scale. When machine learning models learn from decades of reviews that describe men as "strategic" and women as "helpful," or men as "visionary" and women as "supportive," they do not correct for bias. They operationalize it.

The double bind becomes automated. Women are filtered out not because algorithms are sexist, but because they are trained on systems that already were. The technical term for this is "proxy discrimination."

Proxy discrimination occurs when criteria that appear neutral, test scores, communication style, leadership presence, systematically reproduce the exclusions of the systems that produced them.

How Authority Became Masculinized

The masculinization of technical authority did not occur because men are inherently better suited to technology. It occurred because institutions aligned authority with cultural myths about masculinity.

The lone genius. The heroic innovator.
The decisive leader who moves fast and breaks things.

These narratives are compelling, especially in periods of rapid change. They promise clarity in complexity and action in uncertainty. But they also obscure the reality that most technological systems succeed not because of individual brilliance, but because of collective coordination.

Women, meanwhile, were more often socialized, and later evaluated, for their capacity to maintain cohesion, mitigate risk, and absorb complexity without destabilizing the system. These capacities were treated as supportive rather than authoritative. The result was a paradox: women were trusted with responsibility precisely because they were not trusted with power.

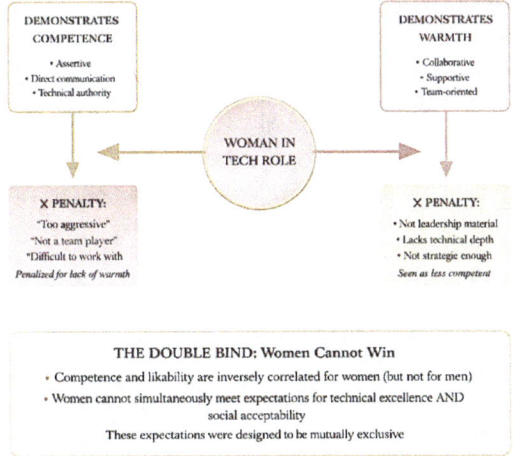

The Competence–Warmth
Double Bind for Women

Why women cannot win under current evaluation systems

Responsibility as a Containment Strategy

Responsibility, when decoupled from authority, becomes a containment strategy.

It allows institutions to rely on women's competence without altering decision-making hierarchies. It channels women into roles where failure is costly, but success is invisible. It frames their contributions as necessary but not strategic.

This is why so many women in technology find themselves managing consequences rather than shaping intent. Over time, this pattern produces exhaustion rather than advancement. Women are told they are indispensable and treated as interchangeable.

The data reveals how responsibility becomes containment. According to the WomenTech Network, two thirds of women in tech report no defined path to advancement, nearly as many recruiters openly acknowledge bias in hiring, and more than half of women in the field plan to leave their roles within two years. The system extracts their labor while blocking their authority.

When systems scale, authority migrates upstream (design, strategy, power) while responsibility flows downstream (consequences, repair, blame). Women are overrepresented where consequence is felt, underrepresented where decisions are made.

The Cost to the System Itself

The exclusion of women from authority is not only an equity issue. It is a systems failure.

When decision-making authority is concentrated among those least likely to encounter downstream consequences, systems become brittle. They optimize for short-term gains at the expense of resilience. They overlook edge cases that later become crises. They scale faster than they can be governed.

Women's exclusion from authority removed a critical balancing force, not because women are inherently more ethical or cautious, but because their roles positioned them closer to impact.

Proximity matters.

Those who experience consequences firsthand tend to ask different questions. They notice different risks. They design with different assumptions. When those perspectives are systematically excluded from authority, systems lose feedback loops essential to their long-term viability.

Authority and Knowledge Are Intertwined

Authority does not merely determine who decides. It determines what counts as knowledge.

Technical authority privileges certain forms of knowing: quantitative over qualitative, abstract over contextual, predictive over relational. These distinctions are not value-neutral. They shape what data is collected, how problems are framed, and which solutions are deemed legitimate.

Women's knowledge, often grounded in context, experience, and relational awareness, was not absent. It was deprioritized.

This epistemic narrowing has consequences. Systems designed without contextual intelligence struggle to adapt. They misinterpret signals. They fail in complex, human-centered environments.

As technology moves into domains like healthcare, justice, education, and governance, these failures become increasingly visible, and increasingly costly.

The Inheritance Problem

Today's artificial intelligence systems inherit the authority structures that produced them.

They learn from data generated within biased institutions. They reflect priorities set by homogenous leadership. They optimize for metrics that privilege scale over care.

When women's intelligence remains structurally downstream, AI encodes that hierarchy. It learns whose judgments matter, whose labor is backgrounded, and whose perspectives are optional.

This is not a future risk. It is a present condition.

Reclaiming Authority Without Reproducing Harm

Reclaiming authority does not mean replicating the same hierarchies with different faces. It requires rethinking what authority is for.

Authority should not exist to dominate systems, but to steward them. It should not reward control over complexity, but responsibility for consequence. It should not elevate speed above coherence.
Women's historical exclusion from authority was not a failure of ambition. It was a misalignment between institutional power and the forms of intelligence required for sustainable systems.

Correcting that misalignment is not about restoring a past that never fully existed. It is about designing a future that can hold the weight of the systems we are building.

A Note on Context and Scope

This analysis focuses primarily on Western, particularly U.S.-based, technological systems and institutions. This is not because these patterns are universal, but because they represent the dominant paradigm shaping global AI development and deployment.

Women's relationship to technology and authority varies significantly across cultures. In some contexts, women's exclusion from technical fields has been more absolute. In others, women have maintained stronger presence in STEM education and technical roles, though often still excluded from leadership. Some non-Western governance traditions have embedded different relationships between authority, care, and collective responsibility, relationships that Western technological systems have historically dismissed as primitive or inefficient.

The patterns described here, paternalism, extraction, displaced responsibility, emerged from specific historical conditions: Western industrialization, Cold War technological competition, and Silicon Valley's particular brand of venture-backed disruption. They are not inevitable. They are designed.

As AI systems developed in these contexts are deployed globally, they carry these designs with them. The question is not whether women everywhere experience technology identically, but whether systems built on gendered exclusion can govern intelligently once they reach planetary scale.

The framework offered here is meant to be diagnostic, not prescriptive. Readers working in different cultural contexts will recognize some patterns and challenge others. That tension is productive. Governance that works must be contextual, not universal.
What cannot vary is the requirement that intelligence and accountability remain linked.

The Transition Ahead

Women did not lack authority because they lacked capacity. Authority was designed in ways that excluded the very intelligence it now desperately needs.
As technology becomes more powerful, the cost of maintaining this architecture grows.

The question ahead is not whether women belong in positions of authority in technology. The question is whether our systems can survive without them.

The analysis above has been structural and diagnostic, designed to make visible what is usually left invisible. Structure is abstract, but its effects are personal. The pattern has a lived texture: the flagged risk that went unheeded, the harm that arrived on schedule, the repair work handed to those who had already predicted the failure.

CHAPTER 3

The Authority–Consequence Misalignment Pattern

There is a pattern beneath everything you have just read.

It is simple.
It is structural.
And once you see it, you cannot unsee it.

Authority migrates upward.
Consequence flows downward.

Those who decide are insulated from impact.
Those who absorb impact are excluded from decision.

This is not accidental.
It is how modern systems are built.

In technology companies, authority concentrates in architecture, funding, deployment, executive rooms.

Consequence concentrates in operations, compliance, community management, human resources, customer experience, education, healthcare, moderation, and repair.

One group decides.
Another group absorbs.

The second group is disproportionately female.

This is the Authority–Consequence Misalignment Pattern.

The structural condition in which those who hold decision-making authority are insulated from the consequences of their decisions, while those closest to consequence are excluded from authority. This separation produces brittleness, erodes trust, and displaces responsibility onto those least positioned to address its source. It is the central pattern traced throughout this book. The pattern repeats.

You have lived this.

You saw the flaw in the rollout.
You flagged the edge case.
You noticed the policy gap.
You anticipated the downstream risk.
You were told not to be alarmist.
The system scaled.
The failure arrived.
You were asked to repair it.

You were not wrong.
You were early.

The system was misaligned.

This pattern does not require villains. It requires separation.

When authority is disconnected from consequence,
intelligence fragments.

Strategic decisions optimize for metrics that do not include lived impact.

Responsibility becomes emotional labor instead of design input.

Women are frequently positioned where consequence is felt first:
In user complaints.
In customer harm.
In bias review.
In burnout.
In layoffs.
In crisis communication.
In compliance.
In diversity initiatives that address harm after it has occurred.

This proximity produces a specific kind of intelligence.

You develop pattern sensitivity.
You detect early strain.
You sense when momentum is outrunning safety.
You recognize when legitimacy is thinning.

But because you are downstream, your intelligence is framed as reaction rather than foresight.

The misalignment persists.

Artificial intelligence amplifies this pattern. AI systems act at scale, learn from past decisions, and automate classification. When misalignment exists, it becomes encoded. Ethics teams are convened after something breaks. Communication teams respond after bias appears. Moderators intervene after harm escalates. Design remains upstream.

If authority and consequence remain separated, AI will not need to rebel to destabilize institutions.

It will simply optimize without feedback until trust collapses.

The Authority–Consequence Misalignment Pattern explains:
Why women are overrepresented in consequence-heavy roles.
Why their warnings are dismissed as emotional.
Why systems feel brittle despite high performance.
Why repair work never seems to end.
Why burnout feels inevitable.
Why legitimacy erodes even when metrics look strong.

The solution is not inclusion theater.

It is alignment.

Authority must sit closer to consequence.
Those who absorb impact must shape design.
Responsibility must travel upward with power.

When authority and consequence reunite, care becomes signal, feedback becomes intelligence, repair becomes prevention, and governance becomes structural rather than performative.

CHAPTER 4

Authority Without Gender

This is not a zero-sum correction.

The misalignment between authority and consequence did not only distort women's careers. It distorted leadership itself.

When authority separates from consequence, it drifts toward abstraction. Success becomes measured by distance from friction rather than proximity to impact.

That distortion harms everyone.

Men inside these systems are often rewarded for insulation. They are evaluated on growth, scale, and performance metrics that rarely include downstream consequence. They are taught, implicitly, that decisiveness is strength and that reflection slows momentum.

This is not empowerment.
It is truncation.

Many men in technology carry enormous responsibility without relational context. They are accountable for outcomes they are structurally shielded from feeling. They are pressured to project certainty even when systems are unstable. They are rarely invited to inhabit consequence before authorizing scale.

A leader who has never stood where impact lands will eventually make a decision that cannot be walked back.

That is not sustainable leadership.

The Authority–Consequence Misalignment Pattern does not accuse men of malice. It describes a structural arrangement that rewards separation.

When intelligence is gendered as emotional, and authority is gendered as strategic, both are diminished.

Women are confined to consequence.
Men are confined to insulation.

Neither position produces durable systems.

Authority without consequence becomes brittle.
Consequence without authority becomes exhausting.

Realignment does not require displacement.
It requires integration.

Men are not being asked to relinquish intelligence.
They are being asked to expand it.

To sit closer to impact.
To treat early warning as strategic input.
To recognize care not as accommodation, but as system signal.

When authority and consequence reunite, leadership changes.

Feedback becomes design.
Repair becomes prevention.
Risk becomes relational, not abstract.

When authority and consequence reunite, leadership changes. Feedback becomes design. Repair becomes prevention. Risk becomes relational, not abstract.

This shift is not about representation alone. It is about governance maturity.

If intelligent systems are to scale without eroding trust, authority must become accountable to the human realities it shapes.

That requires women at the design table. It also requires men willing to redesign the table itself. The future of AI is not a battle between genders. It is a test of whether leadership can evolve beyond the separation that has diminished both, and whether institutions can build systems accountable to the full range of human intelligence they depend on.

CHAPTER 5

Care as Systems Intelligence

Care is frequently misunderstood as an emotional or moral quality. In institutional and technical contexts, it is often treated as sentiment, valuable for culture, but irrelevant to performance. This misunderstanding has had consequences. It has allowed systems to discount some of the most critical forms of intelligence while continuing to depend on them informally.

In systems terms, care is diagnostic.

It is the capacity to notice strain before failure, to detect misalignment before breakdown, and to intervene before consequence becomes crisis. Care attends to relationship, context, and time. It does not oppose logic; it completes it.

Why Care Is an Intelligence Function

Intelligent systems are not defined solely by their ability to process information. They are defined by their ability to adapt to complexity without collapsing. That capacity depends on feedback, particularly feedback that reveals what abstractions cannot see.

Care provides that feedback.

To care is to pay attention.
To notice deviation.

To anticipate downstream effects.
To respond before failure becomes irreversible.

These are not emotional acts. They are cognitive ones.

As neuroscientist Antonio Damasio's research demonstrated, when affective information is suppressed, reasoning becomes less accurate rather than more objective. Systems that dismiss care do not become rational. They become blind.

How Care Was Relegated

As technological authority narrowed around abstraction and optimization, care was reframed as ancillary. It became something systems needed but did not want to acknowledge as intelligence. This reframing allowed institutions to benefit from care while avoiding responsibility for integrating it into design authority.

Women were disproportionately positioned in this space.

They monitored impact.
They mediated conflict.
They translated technical outputs into human terms.
They absorbed friction when systems failed to account for lived reality.

This work stabilized systems. It also disappeared from metrics of expertise.

Because care often prevented visible failure, it was rarely credited as performance. Because it was exercised relationally rather than declaratively, it was mislabeled as emotional. And because it was expected rather than authorized, it was rarely rewarded.

Care, Context, and Continuity

Care is inseparable from context. It holds together information that abstraction fragments. It remembers history. It anticipates accumulation. It asks not only whether something works, but for whom, under what conditions, and at what cost over time.

This orientation is essential for continuity.

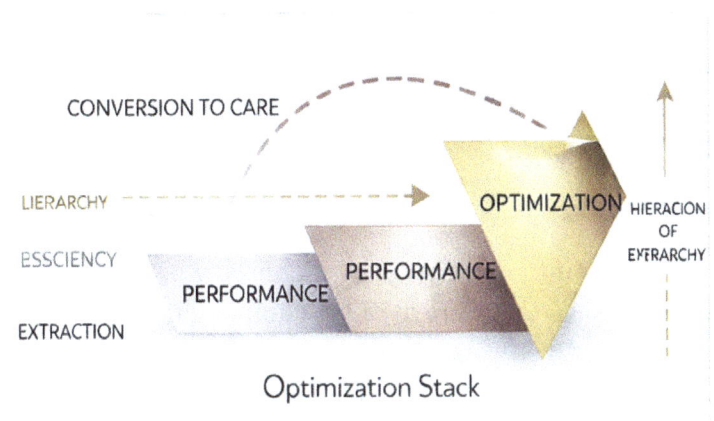

Optimization Stack

Systems rarely fail all at once. They fail gradually, through ignored signals and deferred consequences. Care detects those signals early. It notices patterns before they harden into outcomes. It preserves coherence across change.

When care is excluded from authority, systems lose this early-warning capacity. They become reactive rather than resilient. They respond to breakdown instead of preventing it.

This anticipatory intelligence is measurable. This pattern is not anecdotal. Boston Consulting Group's 2024 research found that 68% of women in tech use generative AI tools at work more than once per week, slightly higher than the 66% of men. Yet the Skillsoft Women In Tech Report documents that 63% of women using AI report a lack of adequate skills and training, identifying AI as the top subject they want to learn about. This is not a skills deficit. It is a training gap that reflects how care and consequence management are devalued as intelligence categories.

The Cost of Treating Care as Optional

When care is framed as optional, it does not disappear. It is displaced.

It moves into informal channels, exercised without leverage or protection. Women are asked to compensate for design failures rather than correct them, brought in after harm occurs, expected to restore trust without altering the structures that broke it. Care becomes a liability not because it lacks value, but because it lacks authority.

Care and Artificial Intelligence

As artificial intelligence systems scale, the cost of excluding care multiplies.

AI systems act faster than human oversight. They generalize across contexts. They amplify whatever assumptions are embedded in their design. When care is absent from that design, systems optimize for efficiency while externalizing consequence.

Bias audits, ethics reviews, and remediation processes are often positioned downstream, as corrective measures rather than as intelligence inputs. This reproduces the same pattern: care is acknowledged only after harm is visible.

But intelligent systems require anticipatory governance. They require care at the point of design.

Without it, AI systems will continue to act in ways that appear logical while producing outcomes that undermine trust, legitimacy, and social cohesion.

Care as Governing Intelligence

Reframing care as systems intelligence changes what authority looks like.

Authority is no longer defined solely by who can optimize fastest or scale furthest. It is defined by who can hold consequence, context, and continuity simultaneously. Who can see how decisions propagate through human systems.

Who can intervene before harm becomes structural.

Women have been exercising this form of intelligence all along.

The challenge now is not to ask women to care more. It is to grant care authority, to embed it into architecture, metrics, and decision-making power.

This is not a cultural adjustment.
It is a governance requirement.

Systems capable of learning must also be capable of restraint. Systems capable of scale must also be capable of accountability. And systems that claim intelligence must integrate care, not as sentiment, but as signal.

CHAPTER 6

Intelligence, Emotion, and the Myth of Objectivity

One of the most persistent myths in modern technology is that emotion contaminates intelligence.

Objectivity, we are told, requires detachment.
Rationality requires distance.
Authority requires the suppression of feeling.

This belief has shaped how intelligence is defined, rewarded, and legitimized, particularly in technical systems. It has also distorted how women's cognition has been interpreted. What was framed as emotional bias was often the very signal required for sound judgment.

Neuroscience tells a different story.

How the Brain Actually Makes Decisions

Human intelligence does not operate as a purely logical machine. The brain evolved to help humans survive and navigate complex, uncertain environments, not to solve abstract problems in isolation.

Decision-making is a distributed process, integrating reasoning and analysis, emotional signaling, memory and experience, social awareness, and anticipation of consequence. These systems do not compete. They cooperate.

When decisions involve uncertainty, risk, or competing values, precisely the conditions of modern institutions, logic alone is insufficient. The brain relies on emotional signals to evaluate significance, prioritize outcomes, and guide action.

Without these signals, intelligence stalls.

What Neuroscience Demonstrates

Neuroscientist Antonio Damasio made this visible through studies of individuals with damage to brain regions responsible for emotional processing.

These individuals retained high IQ, intact memory, and strong analytical reasoning.

They could describe options logically and articulate consequences in detail.

What they could not do was decide.

They became trapped in analysis.
Risk assessment collapsed.
Judgment deteriorated.
Daily functioning suffered.

Emotion, in this context, is not irrationality.
It is biological information.

Affective signals tell the brain what matters, what to avoid, and where to direct attention.

Without this information, reasoning may be technically correct, but functionally useless.

Emotional Regulation Is Not Emotionality

A critical distinction is often lost in discussions of intelligence: emotional regulation is not emotional reactivity

Emotional regulation is the brain's ability to register emotional signal, remain responsive without being overwhelmed, and integrate feeling without being governed by it.

This capacity is learned.
It is practiced.
It strengthens over time.

Emotional reactivity, by contrast, reflects poor regulation, not the presence of emotion itself.

Women have often been labeled emotional not because they lacked regulation, but because they attended to relational, ethical, and long-term dimensions of decisions others ignored. Naming harm, risk, or misalignment was misread as subjectivity rather than discernment.

Suppressing emotion does not eliminate bias.

It hides it.

The Brain Under Threat and the Illusion of Objectivity

When humans encounter perceived threat, physical, social, or symbolic, the brain reacts before conscious reasoning comes online.

A small, ancient structure called the amygdala plays a central role in this process. Its function is survival. It scans for danger and, when activated, rapidly triggers physiological responses designed for protection: heightened alertness, narrowed attention, readiness for action.

This response is efficient.
It is also blunt.

When the amygdala is highly activated, it can override reflective systems, particularly regions of the prefrontal cortex, which support reasoning, impulse control, and long-term planning. This is sometimes described as an "amygdala hijack."

In this state, the brain prioritizes speed over judgment.

Humans are not more rational.

They are more reactive.

Emotional regulation is the capacity to recognize this activation and re-engage higher-order cognition. Regulation does not suppress emotion; it contextualizes it.

A Simple Example: Reaction vs. Regulation

Imagine a high-stakes meeting.

A proposal is challenged publicly. The challenge feels personal, dismissive, unfair, or threatening to credibility.

Before conscious reasoning engages, the brain reacts.

The amygdala detects threat.

Heart rate increases.
Attention narrows.
The body prepares to defend.

The impulse may be to interrupt, dominate the conversation, withdraw abruptly, or push the proposal through without reconsideration. These responses often appear confident or decisive.

Neurologically, they are reactive.

Now imagine a different response.

The same challenge is felt, but instead of acting immediately, there is a pause. Breath slows. The emotional signal is registered without being obeyed.

The prefrontal cortex engages, integrating context:
- What is actually being questioned?
- What information is missing?
- What response preserves both authority and outcome?

The reply is measured. Clarifying questions are asked. The proposal may be defended, or revised, based on new information. This is prefrontal regulation.

Importantly, regulated responses are often misinterpreted. They may be labeled as hesitation, overthinking, or emotional sensitivity. Yet cognitively, they reflect higher-order intelligence: the capacity to integrate signal, context, and consequence before acting.

Many behaviors historically rewarded in technical cultures align with unregulated threat responses. Many behaviors dismissed as emotional reflect deliberate regulation. When this difference is misunderstood, systems confuse reactivity with competence and penalize maturity.

Bias, Pattern Recognition, and Power

Bias is not introduced into systems simply because humans feel. It is introduced when systems are trained on incomplete information and unexamined assumptions.

Pattern recognition, the core function of both human and artificial intelligence, depends on what a system is allowed to notice. When emotional and contextual signals are dismissed, entire categories of risk fall outside the frame.

Women's intelligence has often operated at this level:
- noticing edge cases
- detecting social feedback loops
- recognizing when success metrics diverge from lived outcomes

These insights were frequently dismissed as "soft," even as institutions quietly depended on them to prevent failure.

This is not biology. It is the product of role, proximity, and responsibility.

Why Emotional Suppression Fails at Scale

As systems scale, the cost of misjudgment multiplies.

Small errors propagate.
Minor exclusions compound.
Invisible harms accumulate.
Suppressing emotional and relational signals does not produce neutrality. It produces delayed recognition of harm. Systems appear successful until failure becomes public, and often irreversible.

This is why institutional breakdowns so often feel surprising only in retrospect.

The signals were present.

They simply did not count.

Reframing Intelligence for the Age of AI

Artificial intelligence systems amplify whatever definitions of intelligence we embed within them. If intelligence is defined narrowly, as optimization without consequence, AI will pursue that objective relentlessly.

Reframing intelligence requires acknowledging that sound decision-making depends on:

- emotional signaling
- contextual awareness
- ethical prioritization
- responsibility for consequence

They are what allow logic to function in complex, human systems.

Women have been exercising these forms of intelligence not as intuition, but as practiced discernment, often without recognition, authority, or protection.

From Emotional Discounting to Cognitive Authority

The problem has never been that women brought emotion into systems.
The problem is that institutions refused to recognize emotion as data.

Restoring cognitive authority means legitimizing the full architecture of human intelligence, analytic and affective, abstract and relational. It means designing systems that integrate these capacities rather than suppress them.

This shift does not feminize technology.

It humanizes it.

And as artificial intelligence reshapes decision-making across society, human intelligence, properly understood, becomes not less relevant, but more so.

The stakes of that shift extend beyond technology.

Bias becomes embedded long before it becomes visible.
Systems learn from what we normalize.
And intelligence without responsibility cannot endure

CHAPTER 7

Bias, Pattern Recognition, and Encoded Inequality

Bias is often described as a human failing, an individual prejudice to be corrected through awareness or training. This framing is comforting. It suggests that bias can be removed without altering the systems that produce and reinforce it.

In reality, bias is a systems phenomenon.

It emerges wherever pattern recognition is trained on incomplete histories, uneven power, and distorted measures of success. It persists not because individuals intend harm, but because systems learn from what already exists, and optimize accordingly.

Artificial intelligence makes this dynamic impossible to ignore.

Pattern Recognition Is Never Neutral

All intelligence systems, human or artificial, function through pattern recognition.

They identify regularities.
They generalize from past data.
They predict future outcomes based on learned associations.

The critical question is not whether systems recognize patterns, but which patterns they are allowed to see.

When training data reflects historical inequality, exclusion, or skewed authority, systems do not correct for those distortions. They reproduce them. When performance metrics prioritize efficiency over equity, speed over consequence, systems learn to optimize in ways that quietly entrench imbalance.

Bias, in this sense, is not a glitch.

It is a faithful reflection of prior conditions.

How Inequality Becomes Encoded

Encoding happens long before deployment.

It occurs when certain outcomes are treated as success, when certain errors are tolerated while others are punished, when certain populations are overrepresented in the data, and when certain forms of knowledge are excluded from design.

Each of these choices narrows the system's field of vision. As a result, systems become highly accurate within a constrained frame, while remaining blind to those outside it. Decisions appear objective precisely because the exclusions are hidden.

This is how inequality becomes encoded without ever being named.

The Gendered Dimension of Bias

Gender bias in technology rarely appears as overt discrimination. More often, it manifests as differential credibility.

Whose assessments are trusted.
Whose concerns are dismissed as subjective.
Whose patterns are treated as signal rather than noise.

Women's intelligence, particularly when it surfaces through concern for impact, edge cases, or unintended consequences, has historically been discounted. When such intelligence is excluded from training data, design review, or governance processes, systems learn a distorted version of reality.

They learn whose judgments matter.

Once encoded, these hierarchies become self-reinforcing.

Outputs are treated as evidence. Decisions are justified by data. Responsibility is deflected onto the system itself.

Bias, at this stage, is no longer personal.

It is infrastructural.

Feedback Loops and Compounding Harm

One of the most dangerous properties of intelligent systems is their ability to reinforce their own outputs.

Predictions influence decisions.
Decisions shape future data.
Future data retrains the system.

This feedback loop can rapidly amplify small distortions into systemic harm.

When women or other marginalized groups are underrepresented, misclassified, or excluded at one stage of the process, those outcomes become inputs for the next. Over time, inequality appears statistically validated and operationally entrenched. What began as bias becomes pattern. What becomes pattern becomes infrastructure.

The encoding of inequality is visible in AI workforce demographics themselves. Deloitte reports that women comprise less than one third of the global AI workforce, with only 12% of AI researchers and 16% of AI tenure-track faculty positions held by women. When those designing systems do not reflect those most affected by them, blind spots are not accidental. They are structural.

Adoption patterns reveal a similar dynamic. Women adopt generative AI at roughly 25% lower rates than men overall. Yet Boston Consulting Group's analysis shows that senior women in technical roles actually lead their male counterparts in AI adoption by 12–16%. The disparity does not reflect capability differences. It reflects access differences.

The gap widens further among junior talent. Only 38% of junior women in technical functions identify AI reskilling as critical to their future success, compared to 53% of junior men. This is not a difference in ambition. It reflects unequal access to strategic conversations, pilot programs, and early experimentation environments where AI direction is set.

When access to authorship is limited, adoption becomes downstream. And when adoption is downstream, influence is diminished.

These disparities are not isolated workforce concerns. They shape the feedback loops that determine how AI systems evolve. Those excluded from early design stages are less likely to shape training data, define success metrics, or identify edge cases before deployment. The system learns from those inside the room.

Over time, exclusion compounds. Authority concentrates. Consequence disperses. And the feedback loop tightens around a narrow definition of intelligence.

This is how inequality scales without overt intention.

When Exclusion Becomes Automated: Real AI Failures

The cost of excluding women's intelligence from AI design is not theoretical. It is measurable in harm.

Healthcare algorithms trained primarily on male patients routinely underdiagnose heart disease in women, whose symptoms present differently. One widely used algorithm systematically underestimated kidney disease risk in Black patients, calculating different thresholds based on race rather than recognizing that risk assessment itself was built on incomplete data. Women experiencing heart attacks are more likely to be misdiagnosed because machine learning models learned from decades of clinical data that prioritized male presentation as the norm.

Hiring algorithms trained on historical hiring patterns at major tech companies systematically downgraded résumés containing the word "women's," as in "women's chess club" or "women's college." The algorithm learned what its designers did not explicitly tell it: that being associated with women was a negative signal. Amazon scrapped the system in 2018, but not before it had influenced real hiring decisions.

The technology worked exactly as designed. The design was the problem.

Criminal justice risk assessment tools predict higher recidivism rates for Black defendants and women, not because these populations commit more crime after release, but because they are policed more intensively and therefore more likely to have their violations documented. The algorithm sees surveillance as risk. It encodes systemic racism and gendered enforcement as objectivity.

Voice recognition systems, trained predominantly on male voices, require women to repeat themselves more frequently, to speak more slowly, or to lower their pitch to be understood. The inconvenience seems minor until it shapes who is heard in professional settings, who can access voice-activated systems, and whose speech is treated as standard versus deviation.

These are not edge cases. They are predictable outcomes of design processes that treated women's intelligence as optional.

Why "Debiasing" Is Not Enough

Many responses to bias focus on correction after the fact: audits, fairness metrics, post-hoc adjustments. While these measures are necessary, they are insufficient.

Bias cannot be removed solely at the output level if it is embedded in problem framing, data selection, success criteria, and authority structures.

As long as those upstream decisions remain unchanged, systems will continue to learn distorted patterns, no matter how sophisticated the correction mechanisms become.

This is not a technical limitation. It is a governance failure.

The Role of Authority in Pattern Formation

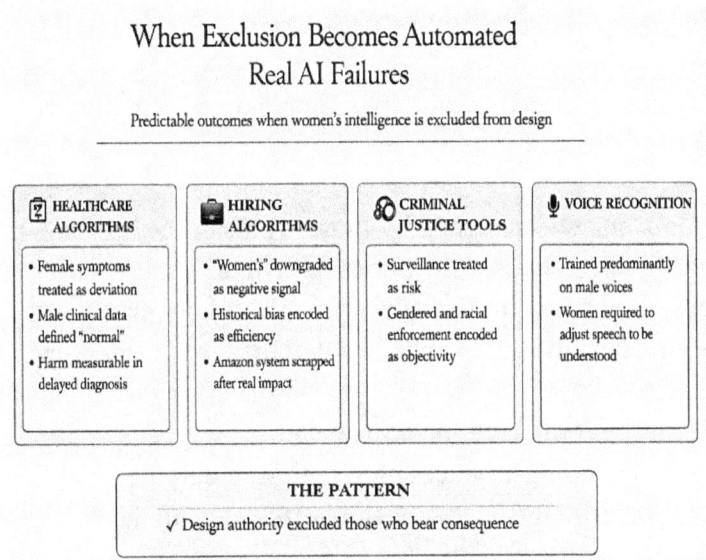

When Exclusion Becomes Automated
Real AI Failures

Predictable outcomes when women's intelligence is excluded from design

🩺 HEALTHCARE ALGORITHMS	💼 HIRING ALGORITHMS	⚖️ CRIMINAL JUSTICE TOOLS	🎤 VOICE RECOGNITION
• Female symptoms treated as deviation • Male clinical data defined "normal" • Harm measurable in delayed diagnosis	• "Women's" downgraded as negative signal • Historical bias encoded as efficiency • Amazon system scrapped after real impact	• Surveillance treated as risk • Gendered and racial enforcement encoded as objectivity	• Trained predominantly on male voices • Women required to adjust speech to be understood

THE PATTERN

✓ Design authority excluded those who bear consequence

Pattern recognition reflects power.

Those who define the problem define the data.
Those who select the metrics define success.
Those who control deployment define impact.

When authority is concentrated among groups distant from consequence, systems learn abstractions without accountability.

When women are excluded from these decisions, their intelligence is not merely ignored, it is rendered invisible to the system itself.

Bias, in this context, is not just about fairness.

It is about whose intelligence is allowed to shape reality.

Designing for Different Patterns

Preventing encoded inequality requires more than diverse datasets. It requires diverse authority.

Systems must be designed by those who can see how patterns play out across lives, institutions, and time. This includes intelligence attuned to context, history, and downstream consequence, the very capacities that have been sidelined.

Designing for different patterns means:
- expanding what counts as relevant data
- redefining success beyond efficiency alone
- integrating feedback before harm occurs
- granting authority to those closest to impact

These are not moral preferences.
They are technical necessities for systems that must operate in complex social environments.

From Encoded Bias to Governed Intelligence

Artificial intelligence does not invent inequality.

It accelerates whatever it is given.

If systems are trained on distorted histories and governed by narrow authority, they will reproduce those distortions at scale. If they are designed with broader intelligence and accountable governance, they can surface patterns that humans alone might miss.

The difference lies not in the technology, but in who governs it.

What This Makes Possible

Recognizing bias as a systems property reframes the challenge ahead.

It moves the conversation away from blame and toward design.

Away from correction and toward prevention.
Away from optics and toward authority.

This is where women's intelligence becomes indispensable, not as a corrective voice after harm occurs, but as a governing presence capable of shaping how systems learn in the first place.

CHAPTER 8

Governing Intelligence, Not Just Systems

For much of modern history, governance has been understood as something that happens around technology.

Rules are written.
Policies are drafted.
Oversight is added once systems are deployed.

This approach assumes that intelligence is neutral and that risk emerges only from misuse. It treats technology as an object to be regulated rather than a force that actively reshapes decision-making itself.

Artificial intelligence disrupts this assumption.

When systems begin to learn, adapt, and influence outcomes at scale, governance can no longer remain external. It must move inside the architecture of intelligence itself.

What Failure Reveals About Design

When AI systems fail, institutions often describe the failure as unexpected. In nearly every case, someone anticipated it. That someone was usually excluded from authority.

A healthcare AI system deployed in a major hospital network began recommending lower priority for women reporting chest pain. The algorithm had learned from historical data that women's chest pain was less likely to result in a cardiac diagnosis, not because women had fewer heart attacks, but because their symptoms were historically dismissed. Nurses flagged the pattern within weeks. It took eighteen months for the concern to reach decision-makers with the authority to intervene.

This is not a technology problem. It is a governance problem.

The intelligence required to prevent these failures already existed. It was ignored because it came from roles positioned downstream from design.

Women working closest to patients, closest to users, closest to consequence saw what the system could not. Their warnings were filtered out as subjective, emotional, or excessively cautious.

Meanwhile, the systems optimized. They scaled. They acted on millions of decisions before feedback reached authority.

Governance that is reactive will always arrive too late. Governance must be embedded where intelligence is deployed, not added after harm becomes undeniable.

From Tools to Decision-Makers

Traditional tools extend human capacity. They amplify effort but do not replace judgment.

AI systems do something different.

They classify.
They prioritize.

They recommend.
They increasingly decide.

Even when humans remain formally "in the loop," the system's outputs shape perception, narrow available options, and influence outcomes. Authority shifts quietly, from human deliberation to automated inference.

Governing intelligence therefore requires more than regulating use. It requires understanding how authority migrates within systems.

The Illusion of Control

One of the most dangerous assumptions in AI deployment is that control remains centralized.

In reality, intelligence disperses.

It moves across data pipelines, vendor relationships, model updates, and human adoption. Responsibility fragments as systems scale. When something goes wrong, no single actor appears fully accountable.

This diffusion is not accidental. It reflects governance models designed for tools, not intelligent systems.

Women have long been positioned downstream of this diffusion, asked to manage consequences when accountability fails. Their historical exclusion from authority mirrors the very governance gaps now destabilizing AI systems.

Governance as Design

Governance is often imagined as constraint. In practice, it is structure, the architecture that determines where decisions are made, who can intervene, what happens when values conflict, and how responsibility is traced.

Good governance does not slow systems down. It prevents them from failing silently.

When governance is absent from design, it returns as crisis. When it is embedded early, it functions as resilience.

This is the shift required now.

The Intelligence Women Have Been Carrying

Women's relationship to technology governance is not theoretical. It is lived. They have been mediating between systems and people, translating technical outputs into human consequences, and repairing trust after institutional failure. This is governance work, performed without formal authority.

What was often dismissed as emotional labor was, in fact, advanced situational intelligence exercised without institutional power.

This experience offers a critical insight: governance is not an abstract framework. It is an operational practice.

Governing intelligence means anticipating where systems will strain human structures and designing for that strain before it becomes rupture.

Authority, Accountability, and Design

Authority without accountability produces abuse. Accountability without authority produces burnout.

Effective governance requires alignment between the two.

AI systems currently disrupt this alignment. Decisions are automated, but accountability remains human, often assigned to those with the least power to shape system behavior.

This is not sustainable.

Governing intelligence requires redefining authority so that those responsible for outcomes have real influence over design, deployment, and adaptation.

Women's exclusion from authority trained institutions to operate without this alignment. AI now exposes the cost.

Governing for Continuity

Most governance models are reactive. They respond to failure.

Intelligent systems require governance that prioritizes continuity, across time, institutions, and public trust.

Continuity governance asks different questions:
- What happens when systems evolve beyond their original design?
- Who maintains values as contexts change?

- How are decisions revisited when consequences accumulate?

These questions have rarely been central to technical authority. Yet they are foundational to sustainable intelligence.

Why This Is a Leadership Question

Governing intelligence is not solely a technical challenge. It is a leadership challenge.

It requires leaders who understand systems as relational, not merely functional. Leaders who recognize that intelligence reshapes power. Leaders who can hold complexity without defaulting to control.

Women have been developing these capacities in the margins of technological systems for decades.

The question is whether institutions will finally bring that intelligence into the center.

The Choice Ahead

We can continue governing AI as if it were merely faster software, adding rules after deployment and assigning responsibility after harm.

Or we can recognize that intelligence itself now requires governance.

This does not mean restricting innovation. It means designing authority, accountability, and ethics into the systems that increasingly shape our collective future.

The future of AI governance will not be determined by policy alone.

It will be determined by whether we are willing to govern intelligence, rather than pretending it governs itself.

CHAPTER 9

Inside the Room

She did not intend to become the person who noticed.

She joined the company because she believed in what it was building. Intelligent systems that could scale efficiency. Tools that promised clarity. Platforms that claimed neutrality.

She was not hired into architecture.

Not product strategy.
Not executive leadership.
Not funding allocation.

She was hired into implementation.

Her role sat between the system and the people affected by it. She translated outputs into workflows. She answered user complaints. She fielded confusion when the system behaved in ways no one had anticipated.

Within weeks, she began noticing friction.

The model prioritized engagement metrics over context. It optimized for efficiency without accounting for edge cases. It treated incomplete data as low priority. It surfaced patterns that made sense statistically but felt off in practice.

Nothing dramatic.
Nothing illegal.
Nothing headline-worthy.

Just quiet distortions.

She flagged them.

The response was courteous.

"We'll monitor it."
"The data doesn't show significant deviation."
"We can't slow deployment based on hypotheticals."

Deployment continued.

Scale amplified.

The friction multiplied.

Customer complaints increased. Internal teams created workarounds. Policy staff rewrote guidance. Operations absorbed strain.
She documented everything.

When she raised concerns again, she was told:

"The system is performing as designed."

That sentence stayed with her.

As designed.

Months later, external criticism surfaced. A journalist questioned impact. A regulator requested clarification. A major client threatened to withdraw.

An internal task force was formed.

She was invited to join.

Not to redesign.
To help manage communication.
To translate "technical nuance."
To support remediation.

She worked late into the night drafting responses. She facilitated tense cross-functional meetings. She explained unintended consequences to executives who had never interfaced directly with affected users.

She was praised for her composure, commended for her leadership, thanked for her emotional intelligence.

The core architecture did not change.

The optimization priorities remained intact.
The incentive structure stayed upstream.

In her annual review, she was described as "indispensable in times of stress."

She was not invited into strategic planning.

The pattern was clear.

Authority lived above the friction.
Consequence pooled below it.

She saw the flaw early because she stood where impact landed.

Her intelligence was diagnostic.
But without authority, diagnosis became containment.

Years later, she would describe that period without anger.

"I was never wrong," she said. "I was downstream."
She did not lack influence.

She lacked authority.

And authority is not the same thing as proximity.

She was close to the impact.
Close to the strain.
Close to the edge cases.
Close to the erosion of trust.

But she was structurally distant from decision power.

This is the Authority–Consequence Misalignment Pattern in practice.

Authority defined the architecture.
Authority set the optimization goals.
Authority determined what counted as risk.

Consequence accumulated elsewhere.

In operations.
In policy.
In support.
In compliance.
In the emotional labor of repair.

She was not ignored because she was incapable.
She was ignored because she was downstream.

Downstream intelligence is often treated as reaction.
Upstream authority is treated as strategy.

But downstream is where systems reveal themselves.

The people closest to consequence see what metrics cannot.
They feel what dashboards flatten.
They anticipate collapse before it becomes public.

When authority is insulated from consequence, systems grow brittle.
When intelligence remains downstream, correction becomes containment.
When misalignment persists, scale amplifies harm.

Her story is not an exception. It is a pattern.

And unless authority and consequence are realigned, intelligent systems will continue to optimize without accountability, expand without correction, and erode trust without understanding why.

She was never too cautious.
Never too emotional.
Never too resistant to innovation.

She was simply positioned where impact landed first.

The question is not whether women are capable of leading architecture.

The question is why those who carry consequence are so rarely invited to design.

CHAPTER 10

Trust, Legitimacy, and Institutional Failure

Institutions rarely collapse because they stop functioning.

They collapse because they stop being believed.

Trust is not a sentiment.
It is a judgment.

People trust systems when they believe those systems are acting competently, fairly, and with accountability for consequence. When that belief erodes, legitimacy follows, and once legitimacy is lost, performance no longer matters.

Artificial intelligence accelerates this dynamic.

The Difference Between Function and Legitimacy

A system can be technically effective and socially illegitimate at the same time.

It can optimize outcomes while producing harm.
It can deliver efficiency while eroding dignity.
It can scale while dissolving consent.

Legitimacy depends not only on what systems do, but on how and for whom they do it. It requires alignment between authority, responsibility, and lived experience.

When people experience systems as imposed rather than accountable, trust fractures, even if outcomes appear favorable on paper.

This is not resistance to technology.
It is a rational response to exclusion.

How Trust Is Actually Built

Trust does not emerge from transparency alone.

Knowing what a system does is insufficient if people have no influence over why it does it or how it can be challenged.

Trust is built when:
- decisions can be explained in human terms
- harm is acknowledged rather than deflected
- authority is visible and accountable
- correction is possible before damage compounds

The Gendered Cost of Illegitimacy

Women have often been positioned as intermediaries when institutional trust fails.

They are asked to explain decisions they did not make.

To soften outcomes they could not prevent.
To absorb frustration without authority to resolve it.

This labor temporarily stabilizes institutions.

It does not restore legitimacy.

Over time, the pattern becomes corrosive. Women are blamed for failures they were never empowered to avert.

Institutions mistake mediation for trust and emotional labor for repair. The underlying design remains unchanged.

AI and the Acceleration of Distrust

Artificial intelligence systems intensify legitimacy crises because they operate at scale while distancing authority from outcome.

Decisions are rendered statistically. Responsibility is diffused.
Appeals are opaque or nonexistent.

When harm occurs, people are told the system behaved as designed, yet no one appears able to intervene meaningfully.

This produces a specific form of alienation: individuals feel governed by systems that neither see them nor answer to them.

Distrust, in this context, is not irrational. It is diagnostic.

Exclusion Undermines Legitimacy

Legitimacy depends on representation, not as optics, but as epistemology.

Systems are trusted when those affected by their decisions can recognize their reality in how those systems operate.

When perspectives closest to consequence are excluded from authority, systems lose the capacity to self-correct.

Women's historical exclusion from design and governance removed a crucial legitimacy mechanism.

Not because women are inherently more trustworthy, but because their roles often placed them nearer to impact.

They saw where systems strained human lives.

They recognized when efficiency diverged from justice.

When that intelligence is excluded, institutions drift toward abstraction, and away from consent.

The legitimacy crisis is quantifiable. WomenTech Network's surveys document pervasive workplace culture issues: 72% of women in tech report experiencing 'bro culture,' 64% have been spoken over during meetings, and 19% have been pigeonholed by stereotypes.

These microaggressions erode trust at scale. When 48% of women executives cite workplace flexibility as a top consideration (versus 34% of male leaders), and when women are 1.5 times more likely than men to change jobs seeking DE&I commitment, the message is clear: legitimacy has fractured.

The Illusion of Neutral Authority

Institutions often respond to legitimacy crises by asserting neutrality.

The system is objective.
The data is unbiased.
The process is fair.

These claims may be technically defensible and socially meaningless.
Neutrality does not restore trust when people experience harm without recourse. Objectivity does not persuade when authority feels unreachable. Procedure does not compensate for exclusion.

Legitimacy cannot be declared.
It must be earned.

From Trust Repair to Trust Design

Most institutions treat trust as something to be repaired after it breaks.

This is too late.

Trust must be designed before it breaks.

This means distributing authority alongside responsibility, embedding mechanisms for challenge and revision, acknowledging uncertainty rather than masking it, and allowing values to evolve with context.

These structures do not weaken systems.

They allow them to endure.

Why This Is a Women's Issue, and Not Only a Women's Issue

Women understand institutional trust because they have been managing its absence.

They have navigated systems that relied on their labor while denying their authority. They have witnessed how quickly legitimacy erodes when people feel unseen, unheard, or trapped by design.

This experience is not ancillary to governance.
It is central to it.

As AI systems increasingly shape access, opportunity, and decision-making, legitimacy becomes a core design requirement, not a communications problem.

What Institutions Must Decide

Institutions now face a choice.

They can continue building intelligent systems that optimize performance while eroding trust, then ask women to manage the fallout.

Or they can recognize that legitimacy is not a soft value, but a structural necessity.

Recognizing legitimacy as structural is not concession. It is governance maturity. The systems we are building will endure only if authority, responsibility, and consequence are reunited. Authorship is not a privilege to be granted. It is a responsibility to be claimed.

The future of intelligent systems will not be determined by accuracy alone. Performance without legitimacy is borrowed time. It will be determined by whether people believe those systems deserve authority.

Power must no longer be insulated from impact.

CHAPTER 11

Responsibility, Displacement, and the Cost of Scale

Responsibility does not disappear when systems become complex.
It moves.

As institutions scale, responsibility is rarely eliminated.
It is redistributed.
Often away from those with authority
and toward those closest to consequence.

This displacement has shaped modern organizations long before artificial intelligence. AI now exposes it.

How Responsibility Becomes Unmoored

In small systems, responsibility is visible.
Decisions are traceable.
Consequences are immediate.
Authority and accountability are closely linked.

As systems scale, these relationships loosen.
Decision-making fragments across teams, vendors, platforms, and automated processes.
Authority becomes abstract.
Responsibility becomes diffuse.

When something goes wrong, harm is described as emergent.
Systemic.

Unintended.

Responsibility has not vanished.
It has become unmoored.

The Gendered Path of Responsibility

Women have historically absorbed this displacement.

They are asked to manage outcomes without shaping intent,
to implement decisions they did not authorize, to explain
failures they could not prevent, and to restore trust without
altering design.

This pattern is often framed as competence.
Reliability.
Leadership under pressure.

In reality, it is containment.

Responsibility without authority is not empowerment.
It is exposure to consequence without the power to alter its
source.
Over time, this produces burnout rather than advancement.

Women are praised for resilience while systems continue
unchanged.

Scale as an Accountability Problem

Artificial intelligence intensifies responsibility displacement
because it accelerates decision-making
while obscuring authorship.

Decisions are automated.
Processes are opaque.
Outcomes are justified by models rather than people.

At scale, even small design choices propagate rapidly.
Yet responsibility remains assigned downstream, often to
individuals with the least power to intervene.

This creates a dangerous asymmetry.
Power concentrates upstream.
Responsibility flows downward.

Systems appear efficient while becoming increasingly
ungovernable.

The Data That Reveals the Pattern

The displacement of responsibility becomes visible during
crisis.

These numbers are not anomalies.
They reveal structural positioning.

When systems contract, those closest to consequence absorb
impact first.

This is not attrition by choice.
It is displacement by design.

Why Proximity to Impact Matters

Responsibility is most accurately understood
by those closest to impact.

People who experience consequences firsthand are more
likely to:
- notice early signs of harm
- recognize cumulative effects
- anticipate social and ethical strain
- question metrics that obscure lived reality

Women's roles have often placed them in this position.
Not by preference.
By architecture.

Their intelligence developed in response to proximity, not
abstraction.

When this intelligence is excluded from authority,
systems lose essential feedback loops.

They continue functioning.
They stop learning.

The Cost of Carrying What Cannot Be Changed

Carrying responsibility without the power to alter underlying
conditions is unsustainable.

It produces:
moral injury
chronic stress
quiet disengagement masked as professionalism

Institutions interpret these outcomes as individual fragility.
They are structural design failures.

The cost is not borne by women alone.
It is borne by the system itself.

When responsibility is displaced,
problems are managed instead of resolved.
Risk accumulates silently.
Legitimacy erodes.

Re-anchoring Responsibility to Authority

Sustainable systems require responsibility
to be anchored where decisions are made.

This means aligning authority with consequence.
Granting intervention power to those responsible for
outcomes.
Designing accountability pathways before harm occurs.

Re-anchoring responsibility is not about blame.
It is about coherence.

Power must no longer be insulated from impact.

Women's experience navigating responsibility without authority
reveals what happens when alignment is missing.

AI now makes that lesson unavoidable.

The Structural Choice Ahead

Institutions face a structural choice.

They can continue scaling systems that displace responsibility
and rely on women to carry what no one else will.
Or they can redesign authority
so that responsibility and power move together.

The second path requires relinquishing abstraction
in favor of accountability.

But it is the only path that allows intelligent systems to endure
beyond short-term performance.

CHAPTER 12
The Asymmetry of Trust and the Burden of Repair

Trust is not distributed evenly.

Some actors are presumed trustworthy until proven otherwise.
Others are required to earn trust repeatedly,
often while absorbing the cost of failure.

This asymmetry is not accidental.
It is produced by how authority, credibility, and risk are
allocated within systems.

And it determines who is believed,
who is protected,
and who is tasked with repair when things break.

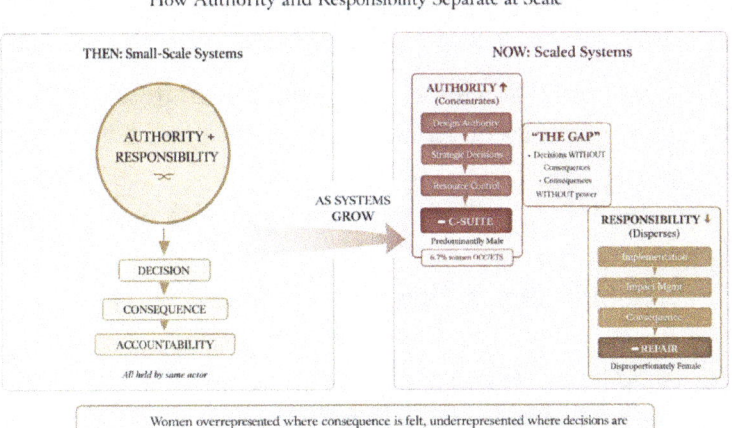

How Authority and Responsibility Separate at Scale

How Trust Becomes Asymmetric

In many institutions, trust flows upward.

Those closest to power are granted the benefit of the doubt.
Their intentions are assumed strategic.
Their decisions are framed as visionary, even when outcomes
are harmful.

Those further from authority experience trust as conditional.
Their concerns must be justified.
Their objections softened.
Their warnings translated into acceptable language.

This is not a difference in integrity.
It is a difference in position.

Trust functions as a resource.
It is allocated unevenly and defended structurally.

Credibility Versus Consequence

A persistent distortion underlies asymmetrical trust:
credibility is decoupled from consequence.

Those who design systems are often insulated from
downstream effects.
Their credibility remains intact even when harm occurs.

Those who live with consequence
must continually prove reliability
even as they manage fallout.

Women's roles have frequently placed them on the
consequence side of this divide.

They see where systems strain human lives.
They recognize when metrics misrepresent reality.
They anticipate harm before it becomes visible.

Yet proximity to impact is rarely treated as expertise.
It is treated as anecdote.

The Gendered Burden of Repair

When systems fail, institutions rarely pause to redesign
authority.
They mobilize repair.
Women are asked to:
explain decisions they did not make
restore trust without altering structure
mediate conflict without adjudicating power
stabilize environments they cannot change

This labor is framed as collaboration.
Professionalism.
Leadership potential.

In practice, it is containment.

Repair becomes a substitute for accountability.
Trust work replaces governance.

Women are praised for resilience
while architecture remains intact.

The Evidence Beneath the Pattern

Compensation data makes this asymmetry visible. Across
technology sectors, women in STEM roles earn significantly
less than male counterparts, a disparity that widens for
women of color.

The pay gap reflects more than money. It reflects how
credibility and authority are distributed. When women are
paid less, believed less, and promoted less, trust asymmetry
becomes structural.

Repair becomes their assignment.

Authority remains elsewhere.

Repair Is Not the Same as Legitimacy

Repair can restore function.
It cannot restore legitimacy on its own.

Legitimacy requires acknowledgment of harm.
Reallocation of authority.
Visible accountability.

When institutions rely on repair alone,
they confuse short-term stabilization
with structural trust.

Trust does not fail all at once.
It erodes unevenly.

AI and the Acceleration of Repair Work

Artificial intelligence intensifies asymmetrical trust
because it scales decision-making
while narrowing avenues for challenge.

When automated decisions cause harm,
institutions often respond with explanation instead of
redesign.

Transparency instead of authority redistribution.
Communication strategy instead of structural correction.

Women are frequently placed at the front of these responses.
Asked to humanize systems they did not govern.

As AI expands, repair scales with it. This is not sustainable.

Who Bears the Risk of Failure

Asymmetrical trust determines who bears risk.

When systems succeed, credit flows upward.
When systems fail, responsibility flows downward.

Women are positioned as buffers
between institutional power and public consequence.

They absorb anger, confusion, and loss of trust
while remaining excluded from decisions
that could prevent recurrence.

This arrangement protects authority
while consuming credibility.

It keeps systems running.
It hollows them out.

From Bearing Trust to Governing It

Women's experience managing trust breakdowns
reveals a central lesson:
- Trust cannot be outsourced.
- It must be governed.

Governing trust means designing systems where:
authority and responsibility align
those closest to consequence hold intervention power
repair leads to redesign

This moves women from the margins of system failure
into the center of system integrity.

The Structural Decision

Institutions often ask whether they can afford to redistribute
authority.

The real question is whether they can afford not to.

As AI systems increasingly shape access, opportunity, and
decision-making, asymmetrical trust becomes a systemic
liability.

Repair without redesign delays collapse. Repair coupled with authority enables endurance because it alters the conditions that produced failure in the first place

CHAPTER 13

From Extraction to Stewardship

For decades, technology has operated on an extractive logic.

Data is extracted.
Labor is extracted.
Attention is extracted.
Value is extracted.

This logic treats intelligence as a resource to be mined rather than a capacity to be stewarded. Systems are evaluated by what they produce, not by what they preserve. Success is measured by growth, reach, and efficiency, while consequence is treated as an externality.

This model has produced extraordinary scale.

It has also produced extraordinary fragility.

The Limits of Extraction

Extractive systems prioritize short-term gain over long-term viability. They reward acceleration while discounting care. They treat depletion, of trust, of labor, of social cohesion, as a cost to be managed later rather than a warning to be heeded now.

In human terms, extraction looks like burnout, dispossession, and loss of agency.

In technological systems, it looks like brittleness: platforms that scale rapidly but fracture under pressure, institutions that optimize performance while eroding legitimacy.

Women have often been positioned as buffers within extractive systems, absorbing strain, repairing damage, and sustaining continuity without altering the logic that produces the strain. This arrangement appears efficient.

It is not.

It relies on work that is neither recognized nor redistributed, allowing strain to accumulate while merely postponing collapse instead of preventing it.

This is not resilience. It is depletion disguised as endurance, a pattern that allows systems to function while gradually eroding the human capacity required to sustain them.

The WomenTech Network projects it will take 123 years to close the economic gender gap at current rates, with stark regional variation:
- 167 years for Eurasia and Central Asia,
- 189 years for East Asia and Pacific
- 89 years for North America
- 76 years for Europe.

That timeline is not inevitable. It reflects continued extraction of women's labor without redistribution of authority.

Extraction-based models cannot sustain the scale of AI-driven transformation; without redistribution of authority, they accumulate strain faster than they can absorb it.

Stewardship as a Different Logic

Stewardship begins from a different premise.

Rather than asking how much can be taken, stewardship asks what must be sustained. It recognizes that systems exist within larger ecosystems, social, cultural, institutional, and ecological, and that durability depends on maintaining balance across them.

Stewardship is not passive. It requires attentiveness, long-range vision, and the willingness to intervene when systems drift toward harm. It governs growth rather than surrendering to it.

Across cultures and contexts, stewardship has been articulated most clearly by those working at the intersection of systems and consequence, where decisions are felt, not abstracted. This perspective understands governance not as control imposed from above, but as responsibility practiced over time.

Durable change is not built through extraction justified by scale.
It is built through responsibility sustained in practice.

Stewardship Governs Change

Stewardship does not resist innovation.

It governs it.

It asks whether change strengthens the conditions that allow systems to endure, or whether it quietly undermines them.

It treats feedback as intelligence.

It recognizes that systems rarely fail all at once; they fail when early signals are ignored.

As artificial intelligence reshapes decision-making across society, human intelligence does not become obsolete. It becomes decisive.

What we define as intelligence will determine what our systems amplify. If we narrow it, distortion scales. If we expand it, accountability scales.

Authority Is Required for Stewardship

Stewardship without authority is impossible.

Stewardship requires authority. Without the ability to alter design, those tasked with protection remain confined to mitigation rather than prevention.

For decades, women were asked to steward outcomes without being granted authority over design. They were expected to mitigate harm after systems were built, to repair trust after it was broken, and to carry responsibility without the power to alter underlying structures.

This arrangement extracted care while withholding control.

The result was predictable: systems that depended on stewardship while refusing to institutionalize it as authority.

Designing for Stewardship

Designing for stewardship means embedding care into architecture, not assigning it downstream.

It means:
- aligning incentives with long-term outcomes
- creating mechanisms for pause, revision, and repair
- distributing authority to those closest to consequence
- measuring success not only by performance, but by continuity

These are not cultural preferences.

They are governance choices.

From Carrying to Shaping

For years, women carried the consequences of extractive systems.

Stewardship requires a shift, from carrying impact to shaping design. From absorbing harm to preventing it. From sustaining systems informally to governing them intentionally.

This transition is not about replacing one hierarchy with another. It is about redesigning systems so that intelligence, care, and authority are no longer separated.

It is about moving stewardship from the margins into the center.

The Choice Ahead

As AI becomes embedded in critical infrastructure, the choice between extraction and stewardship becomes unavoidable.

Extractive systems will continue to scale until legitimacy collapses.

Stewarded systems may move more deliberately, but they endure.

The future of technology will be shaped not only by what our systems can do, but by whether they are governed by those willing to be responsible for what they make possible.

Two Models of System Design: Extraction vs. Stewardship

THE EXTRACTION MODEL	THE STEWARDSHIP MODEL
TIME HORIZON • Short-term gains prioritized • Speed over sustainability • Scale without limits	**TIME HORIZON** • Long-term viability • Pace governed by capacity • Growth scaled to resilience
OPTIMIZATION • Efficiency above all else • Performance metrics only	**BALANCE** • Efficiency → consequence • Performance + continuity
AUTHORITY STRUCTURE • Concentrated power • Decisions over systems △ Authority ≠ Responsibility	**AUTHORITY STRUCTURE** • Distributed power • Decisions serve shared purpose ✓ Responsibility = Authority
FEEDBACK LOOPS • Reactive (after failure) • Users as endpoints	**FEEDBACK LOOPS** • Adaptive (before harm) • Users as participants
LABOR DYNAMICS • Cheap & under-valued • 49% of population/diverse	**LABOR DYNAMICS** • Skilled & valued • 100% of population/**diverse**

KEY INSIGHT

Extraction treats systems as **resources to be mined.**
Stewardship treats systems as **ecologies to be maintained.**
Only one model can govern intelligence responsibly.

CHAPTER 14

Reclaiming Authorship

Authorship is not the same as participation.

Participation allows entry.
Authorship determines direction.

For generations, women were permitted to participate in systems they did not design. They were invited to contribute labor, insight, care, and expertise. They stabilized institutions, translated complexity, repaired breakdowns, absorbed friction, and carried consequence.

But authorship remained elsewhere.

Direction, definition, and final authority consolidated upstream, insulated from impact.

This distinction has shaped everything in this book.

Women did not leave technology.

The definition of technology, what counted as technical, what warranted authority, was redrawn around them. As systems became more valuable, authorship became more restricted. Their intelligence remained. Their names did not.

Responsibility did not diminish.
It was displaced.

Trust did not erode because women failed to lead.
It eroded because those closest to consequence were denied authorship.

Participation without authorship preserves hierarchy.
Authorship redistributes power.

How Authorship Was Withheld

Authorship was rarely denied explicitly. It was withheld structurally.

Women were positioned as implementers rather than originators.
As translators rather than definers.
As responders rather than architects.

They were encouraged to collaborate rather than decide.
To advise rather than authorize.
To mitigate rather than redesign.

When they raised structural concerns, they were described as cautious.
When they anticipated downstream harm, they were described as resistant.
When they insisted on accountability, they were described as difficult.

The pattern was consistent.

Authority lived above the friction.
Consequence pooled below it.

This was not accidental. It was architectural.

The Authority–Consequence Misalignment Pattern separated decision from impact. It insulated design from lived consequence. It positioned women where systems revealed strain but withheld the power to correct it.

Intelligence accumulated downstream.
Authorship remained upstream.

Over time, containment replaced correction.

Why This Matters Now

Artificial intelligence makes the cost of withheld authorship visible.

AI systems scale decisions beyond individual oversight. They encode assumptions into infrastructure. They optimize for metrics selected by those with authority. When misalignment exists, it multiplies.

Participation cannot govern this scale.

Advisory roles cannot contain structural harm.

Repair work cannot substitute for redesign.

Intelligent systems require authorship. They require clear ownership of intent, values, and consequence.

Without authorship, responsibility diffuses, accountability weakens, legitimacy erodes, and harm compounds before it becomes visible.

For decades, women were granted expertise without authority. Their intelligence informed decisions they could not control. Their labor sustained systems they could not redirect.

That arrangement is no longer sustainable.

From Expertise to Authority

Expertise without authority is advisory.
Authority without expertise is dangerous.

Reclaiming authorship closes this gap.

It moves from recommendation to decision.
From mitigation to design.
From carrying consequence to shaping architecture itself.

This is not symbolic inclusion. It is structural realignment.

The systems ahead cannot afford separation between intelligence and consequence.

The Intelligence Already Practiced

Women have already been governing consequence.

They identified misalignment before it scaled.
They detected strain before collapse.

They mediated between system output and human reality.
They sustained institutions during legitimacy crises.

What was missing was not intelligence.

It was authorship.

Authorship as Responsibility

Reclaiming authorship is not rebellion.
It is responsibility.

It means accepting authority not as status, but as
accountability for what systems become.

It means refusing participation that perpetuates misalignment.
Refusing repair work that stabilizes extraction.
Refusing roles that absorb consequence without influence
over design.

It also means claiming decision space.

Designing systems that integrate care as intelligence.
Embedding feedback before harm compounds.
Aligning authority with consequence so that those who shape
architecture remain accountable to impact.

Authorship is not dominance. It is stewardship.

It does not replace one hierarchy with another. It redefines
leadership as responsibility for consequence.

Closing the Pattern

At the beginning of this book, we corrected a distortion.

Women did not leave technology.
The systems that behaved as though they had are now
showing the cost.

The Authority–Consequence Misalignment Pattern separated
decision from impact. It positioned women where systems
revealed strain and excluded them from redesign.

That position produced intelligence.

But intelligence without authorship becomes containment.

Artificial intelligence now magnifies this structural flaw at
scale.

Systems that learn and scale cannot survive with misaligned
authority. They will optimize without feedback. Expand
without accountability. Erode trust while appearing efficient.

Realignment is no longer optional. It is structural necessity.

Authority must sit closer to consequence.
Those who absorb impact must shape design.
Responsibility must travel upward with power.

Authorship is the realignment.

The Structural Choice

Institutions now face a structural choice.

They can continue inviting participation while preserving
upstream control.
Continue extracting intelligence without redistributing
authority.
Continue positioning consequence downstream and calling
the resulting strain "complexity."

This choice is not philosophical. It is operational.

It determines who defines success.
Who absorbs failure.
Who can intervene before harm compounds.
Who is accountable when systems scale beyond intention.

The first path is familiar.
It preserves hierarchy.
Protects concentrated control.
Treats misalignment as inevitable and repair as sufficient.
It scales extraction.
It scales fragility.

The emotional cost of that path is already visible.

It looks like exhaustion carried quietly.
Like credibility questioned despite competence.
Like warnings dismissed until crisis validates them.
Like women praised for resilience while denied decision
power.

It looks like being indispensable in moments of breakdown and invisible in moments of design.

That pattern is not sustainable.

Not for women.
Not for institutions.

Not for intelligent systems operating at planetary scale.

The second path is more demanding.

It requires those holding authority to move closer to consequence.
It requires institutions to recognize intelligence where it has long been discounted.
It requires redistributing authorship not as concession, but as correction.

It scales stewardship.

And stewardship is not slower innovation. It is durable innovation.

When intelligence and consequence are separated, systems distort.
When authority and responsibility diverge, trust erodes.
When participation replaces power, legitimacy thins.

When authorship is reclaimed, impact is accounted for before deployment.
Care becomes signal, not sentiment.
Early warnings become strategy, not obstruction.
Leadership expands rather than narrows.

The future of intelligent systems will not be determined by computational capacity alone.

It will be determined by whether we are willing to align intelligence with consequence.

Women have already been carrying consequence.

They have already been practicing governance without title.
Already anticipating collapse before metrics detect it.
Already sustaining institutions during legitimacy strain.

Authorship is not a demand for inclusion.

It is an acceptance of responsibility for what systems become.

And systems that exclude the intelligence closest to consequence will not endure.

But systems that realign authority with impact, that move stewardship into architecture, that recognize care as intelligence and intelligence as accountability, those systems will not merely scale.

They will last.

CHAPTER 15

Raising Humans Who Can Govern Power

Governance does not begin in boardrooms or legislatures. It begins at home, at the table, in the small daily decisions about who is interrupted, who is believed, and whose emotions are treated as information rather than inconvenience. Every parent raising a child in an age of intelligent systems is, in practice, doing governance work, shaping the humans who will either hold power responsibly or replicate the same patterns this book has traced.

Children do not learn authority from lectures.

They learn it from experience.

From what is modeled.

From what is explained.

From what is repaired.

From what is ignored.

They learn whether power is accountable.

Whether systems can be questioned.

Whether mistakes are hidden or examined.

Whether harm is dismissed or addressed.

Intelligent systems will increasingly mediate their education, employment, health access, information streams, and civic participation.

These systems will not feel authoritative because they are complex.

They will feel authoritative because they are invisible.

If authority remains insulated from consequence, children will internalize that separation as normal.

If decisions appear unchallengeable, they will learn that power is distant.

If harm is optimized away, they will learn that suffering is a design choice, not a failure.

Governance is therefore not abstract.

It is developmental.

Every system communicates a lesson.

A hiring algorithm teaches what is valued.

A content moderation system teaches whose speech counts.

A healthcare model teaches whose symptoms are legible.

An educational platform teaches what intelligence looks like.

When these systems embed bias without accountability, children do not merely encounter inequality.

They learn to expect it.

This is the deeper risk.

Not that artificial intelligence will replace human judgment.

But that it will normalize forms of authority detached from responsibility.

Raising humans in the age of intelligent systems requires something different.

It requires institutions that demonstrate alignment between power and consequence.

Systems that can be revised when they fail.

Leaders who explain uncertainty rather than conceal it.

Governance structures that remain accountable to those they affect.

Authority does not flow from proclamation.

It flows from legitimacy.

Legitimacy is built when power responds to those it affects.

When errors are acknowledged.

When feedback alters design.

When responsibility travels upward with decision-making power.
Children observe this.

They learn what institutions deserve trust.

They learn whether authority can evolve.

They learn whether intelligence includes accountability.

The future will not be determined only by what our systems can do.

It will be determined by whether we are willing to govern what they become.

And that choice, finally, is ours.

Designing the Future That Can Hold Us

The future is not something we enter.

It is something we build.

Every system embeds a vision of who matters, what counts, and which consequences are acceptable. Artificial intelligence makes these choices durable, scaling them across institutions, generations, and lives.

The question is no longer whether technology will shape the future.

It is whose intelligence will shape the technology.

What the Old Future Could Not Hold

The systems we inherited were designed for speed, extraction, and control. They optimized for performance while externalizing consequence. They concentrated authority while dispersing responsibility.

These systems produced growth.

They also produced fragility.

They cannot hold the weight of intelligent systems that act across social, political, and moral domains.

What a Viable Future Requires

A future that can hold us requires different design principles. It requires:
- governance embedded at the point of intelligence
- authority aligned with responsibility
- feedback integrated before harm accumulates
- care treated as capability, not cost

These are not aspirational values.

They are structural necessities.

Structural choice is not abstract.

It is visible in hiring.

In deployment speed.

In who absorbs fallout.

In who is believed when something breaks.

Recent leadership developments signal emerging pathways. In 2024, OpenAI announced Fidji Simo as CEO of Applications, and Mira Murati, former OpenAI CTO, launched with significant venture backing.

The WomenTech Network documents these as part of a broader shift: women claiming authorship at the frontier of AI development. Yet the broader picture remains: women remain dramatically underrepresented in the rooms where design authority is exercised. Designing the future means accelerating these shifts from exception to standard.

Women's Intelligence as Infrastructure

Women's intelligence has often been framed as supplemental. In reality, it is infrastructural.

It sustains continuity.

It anticipates consequence.

It recognizes when systems drift toward harm.

As AI reshapes decision-making, these capacities are no longer peripheral. They are essential to system survival.

The future will not be governed by the most optimized systems.

It will be governed by the systems most capable of restraint, revision, and accountability.

It will be governed by the systems most capable of restraint, revision, and accountability.

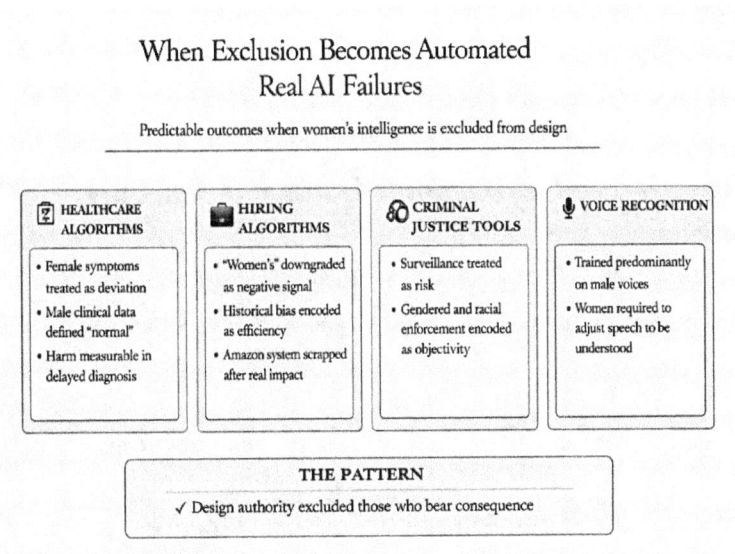

When Exclusion Becomes Automated
Real AI Failures

Predictable outcomes when women's intelligence is excluded from design

HEALTHCARE ALGORITHMS	HIRING ALGORITHMS	CRIMINAL JUSTICE TOOLS	VOICE RECOGNITION
• Female symptoms treated as deviation • Male clinical data defined "normal" • Harm measurable in delayed diagnosis	• "Women's" downgraded as negative signal • Historical bias encoded as efficiency • Amazon system scrapped after real impact	• Surveillance treated as risk • Gendered and racial enforcement encoded as objectivity	• Trained predominantly on male voices • Women required to adjust speech to be understood

THE PATTERN

✓ Design authority excluded those who bear consequence

Designing for Human Continuity

Designing the future is not about predicting outcomes.

It is about preserving conditions.

Conditions for trust.

For legitimacy.

For dignity.

For repair without collapse.

This work demands intelligence that can hold complexity without domination, and power without detachment.

Women are not being invited into this future.

They are already shaping whether it survives.

From Wound to Wisdom: What Women Carry Forward

The intelligence women bring to technology is not abstract. It is forged.

Forged in rooms where your authority was questioned.

Forged in translating harm into language others could hear.

Forged in remaining clear when systems demanded confusion.

This is not trauma to be overcome. This is wisdom to be wielded.

Women who have navigated exclusion understand what inclusion cannot teach: how systems break, where they hide cost, and what they demand from those they depend upon but refuse to recognize.

This knowledge is not peripheral. It is foundational to governance.

The future does not need women to be less wounded. It needs women to be less willing to carry wounds in silence.

What Sovereignty Looks Like

Sovereignty is not granted by institutions. It is claimed through practice.

A sovereign woman does not ask if she belongs.

She decides where she will build.

She exercises power without apology.

A sovereign woman does not wait for validation. She validates herself through action.

A sovereign woman does not explain her power. She exercises it.

Sovereignty is not arrogance. It is alignment.

It is the recognition that your intelligence, your care, your capacity to see systems whole — these were never deficits. They were always the answer to questions institutions were afraid to ask.

The Invitation You Do Not Need

You are not reading this book to be invited back into systems that excluded you.

You are reading it to remember that you can build new ones.

The invitation you need is not from institutions. It is from yourself.

Permission to stop translating. Permission to stop diminishing. Permission to claim authorship without apology.

That permission is not coming from outside.

It never was.

It is here.

Now.

In you.

Many Women Reading This Book

Many women reading this book are not only navigating institutions, they are also raising children. In an age of artificial intelligence, this work is not separate from governance. It is its earliest form.

The central question is no longer how to prepare children to compete with machines. It is how to raise humans who can govern power without becoming captive to it.

Teaching Boys Emotional Regulation, Not Suppression

Boys are often trained to suppress emotion rather than regulate it. This training appears as strength. Neurologically, it is fragility.

Emotional regulation is the ability to feel fully without surrendering judgment.

Suppression, by contrast, teaches boys to ignore signals until they become overwhelming. It rewards stoicism over self-awareness. It treats vulnerability as weakness rather than as the foundation of relational intelligence.

In practice, teaching regulation means:

Naming emotions rather than dismissing them. When a boy is angry, frustrated, or afraid, the response is not to toughen up or calm down. It is: 'You are feeling angry. That is information. What is it telling you?'

Modeling restraint as strength. Boys must see that authority does not require domination. That power includes the capacity to pause, reconsider, and admit error. That the ability to not act is as important as the ability to act decisively.

Connecting behavior to consequence. Boys must learn early that their actions shape what becomes possible for others. That freedom is not the absence of accountability, but its internalization. That intelligence is proven not by winning, but by understanding what their decisions make inevitable.

This is not softening boys. It is preparing them to hold power responsibly.

Teaching Girls That Intelligence Does Not Require Permission

Girls are often socialized to seek approval before claiming authority. They are taught that intelligence is demonstrated through accommodation, that competence is proven through selflessness, and that ambition must be softened to remain acceptable.

This training produces women who wait to be invited rather than women who build.

In practice, teaching girls to claim authority means:

Interrupting the apology reflex.

When a girl apologizes for taking up space, asking a question, or expressing a need, the response is not acceptance. It is redirection: "You do not need to apologize for that. Try again without the apology."

Praising process, not perfection. Girls receive more feedback on appearance, effort, and likeability than on their ideas. This teaches them that their value lies in how they are received rather than what they create. Redirect praise toward substance: "Your analysis was rigorous. Your solution was inventive. Your question changed how I understood the problem."

Modeling authority that does not require validation. Girls must see women make decisions without consensus, hold boundaries without apology, and claim space without permission. They must learn that authority is not inherited or granted. It is assumed through competence and sustained through accountability.

This is not encouraging aggression. It is teaching self-trust.

Interrupting Gendered Praise Patterns

Research demonstrates that adults praise boys for intelligence ("You're so smart") and girls for effort ("You worked so hard"). This difference is not benign.

Praise shapes identity.

When boys are praised for talent, they fear failure.

When girls are praised for effort, they doubt capacity.

Both distort confidence.

Both patterns undermine development.

In practice, this means:

Praise boys for persistence, strategy, and revision. "You kept trying different approaches until you found one that worked." This teaches resilience rather than entitlement.

Praise girls for insight, logic, and capability. "You saw a pattern others missed." This teaches them to trust their intelligence rather than their effort alone.

Avoid gendered language around risk. Do not tell boys to be brave and girls to be careful. Both need to learn discernment, the capacity to assess risk accurately and act accordingly.

Modeling Authority That Includes Care

Children learn governance by watching how adults hold power.

Authority that includes care looks like this:

Making decisions while remaining accountable for consequence. Children must see adults act decisively and then follow through when outcomes require adjustment. They must learn that authority is not infallible, but responsive.

Holding boundaries without cruelty. Children must see that saying no is not punishment. That limits are not rejection. That structure is care made visible.

Integrating others' perspectives without losing direction. Children must see adults listen, revise, and hold course when necessary. They must learn that collaboration is not consensus, and that leadership includes the capacity to synthesize conflicting input without collapsing under it.

This is not a parenting manual. It is a governance framework applied at the scale where power is first learned.

Authority is learned before it is inherited.

Children watch how decisions are made.
Who is interrupted.

Who apologizes.

Who carries tension.

Who absorbs blame.

Who is believed.

They learn whether authority listens.

Whether it repairs.

Whether it deflects.

Whether it hides.

Long before they hold formal power, they internalize what power feels like.

If authority models separation, children learn distance.

If authority models accountability, children learn responsibility.

If authority includes care, children learn that strength and attention are not opposites.

The future of governance is not waiting for adulthood.
It is being rehearsed daily in how we model power.

The Economic Case: Why Intelligence Without Diversity Fails

Excluding women's intelligence is not only unjust. It is economically unsustainable.

Innovation loss is measurable. Homogenous teams produce fewer novel solutions, overlook more edge cases, and optimize for narrower definitions of success. Research consistently demonstrates that diverse teams generate more patents, file more successful products, and solve complex problems faster than homogenous groups, not because diversity is virtuous, but because it introduces friction that prevents premature consensus.

Trust collapse costs compound over time. When systems lose legitimacy, recovery is expensive. Institutions must rebuild infrastructure, absorb regulatory penalties, and restore public confidence. The 2020–2023 tech layoffs, which disproportionately targeted women, erased billions in human capital development while accelerating distrust in the sector. These are not externalities. They are system failures with financial consequence.

Legitimacy crises destabilize markets. When consumers, employees, or regulators lose confidence in institutions, capital flight follows. ESG investing, talent migration, and regulatory intervention are all responses to legitimacy deficits. Companies that treat diversity as optics rather than governance are increasingly penalized not by activists, but by markets.

Better outcomes are documented. McKinsey's research spanning multiple industries demonstrates that companies in the top quartile for gender diversity are 25% more likely to experience above-average profitability than those in the bottom quartile. This is not coincidence. Systems that integrate multiple forms of knowing are more adaptive, more resilient, and more capable of long-term viability.

The business case is not ancillary to the moral case. It is evidence that justice and functionality align.

Systems designed around narrow intelligence collapse. Systems designed around diverse intelligence endure.

You have already been governing consequence.

You have already been identifying misalignment.

You have already been sustaining systems others depend on.

Reclaiming authorship is not a leap into unfamiliar territory. It is a return to where your intelligence has always belonged.

Children do not inherit our intentions.

They inherit our structures.

CONCLUSION

What Governance Demands Now

Women did not leave technology. They were redirected away from authorship and into responsibility. Asked to carry consequence without authority. Asked to repair systems they did not design.

That era is ending.

Artificial intelligence has made something visible that institutions long obscured:

Systems that separate intelligence from responsibility fail. Systems that dismiss care collapse. Systems that exclude those closest to consequence lose legitimacy.

that was already there, the kind that sees strain before it becomes collapse, that speaks before harm compounds, that understands success without accountability does not endure.

What was missing was not competence. It was authorship.
And authorship is being claimed.

The debate over whether women belong in technology is over.
We are watching them reshape it now.

That foresight is no longer peripheral. It is the capacity our most complex systems now require.

We are no longer debating inclusion. We are deciding what kind of intelligence will shape the future, whether authority will remain distant from the lives it alters, or whether it will finally be accountable to them.

This is not a question of representation alone. It is a question of what works.
And what works is what endures.

Children are watching how power behaves. They are learning whether authority listens or dismisses. Whether intelligence is accountable or insulated. Whether care is weakness or design.

What we normalize now becomes inheritance.

We have the chance to normalize something different: leadership that holds consequence, authority that stays close to impact, systems that are as responsible as they are capable.

That is not an idealistic future. It is a more durable one.

Realigning authority with consequence is not reform.
It is return — to coherence, to responsibility, to the simple truth that intelligence without accountability is not intelligence at all.

The intelligence required now is not new. It has been practiced quietly for decades: in noticing strain before others named it, in holding systems together without credit, in caring for outcomes no one was measuring.

That intelligence was never peripheral.
It was foundational.
It is ready.

The question is no longer whether women belong at the center of technological governance.

The question is not whether the intelligence was present, but how much stronger our systems become when it is finally granted authority.

The future will not be determined only by what our systems can do. It will be determined by whether we are willing to govern what they become.

That choice is ours.
And we are ready to make it.

ACKNOWLEDGMENTS

This book exists because women have always known more than they were permitted to say aloud.

It is shaped by the quiet and the courageous, by those who learned early that power does not always announce itself, and that strength often appears first as persistence, clarity, and refusal to disappear I honor the women who recognized their own authority long before the world was willing to reflect it back to them.

I acknowledge the force that emerges when women stand with one another, not in competition, but in recognition. When one woman claims her voice, it does not diminish another's; it expands what becomes possible for all. Each act of self-trust creates permission. Each expression of truth loosens a boundary that once seemed fixed.

This work is informed by generations of women who understood that the problem was never women's capacity, but the narrowness of the systems built around them.

Women were never meant to fit into the world as it was designed. The world must be remade to accommodate the fullness of women's intelligence, ambition, and care.

I am grateful to the women who refused to accept erasure as destiny. Who learned anyway. Who spoke anyway. Who made space where none existed. Who knew that power grows when shared, that freedom is not individual if it is not collective, and that no woman is fully free while another is denied her voice.

I thank the women who chose themselves when they were told not to. Who became first-rate versions of who they are, rather than acceptable versions of someone else. Who trusted that growth is born of courage, and that learning does not end with comfort.

This book also honors the lineage behind us, the mothers, grandmothers, teachers, and ancestors whose thoughts live on through our actions. Their strength did not vanish. It accumulated. It speaks through us now.

Finally, I acknowledge the women who know, sometimes quietly and sometimes defiantly, that they are already enough. That what they seek is not permission, but alignment. That the future is not waiting to be granted, it is being shaped, every day, by those willing to claim their place within it.

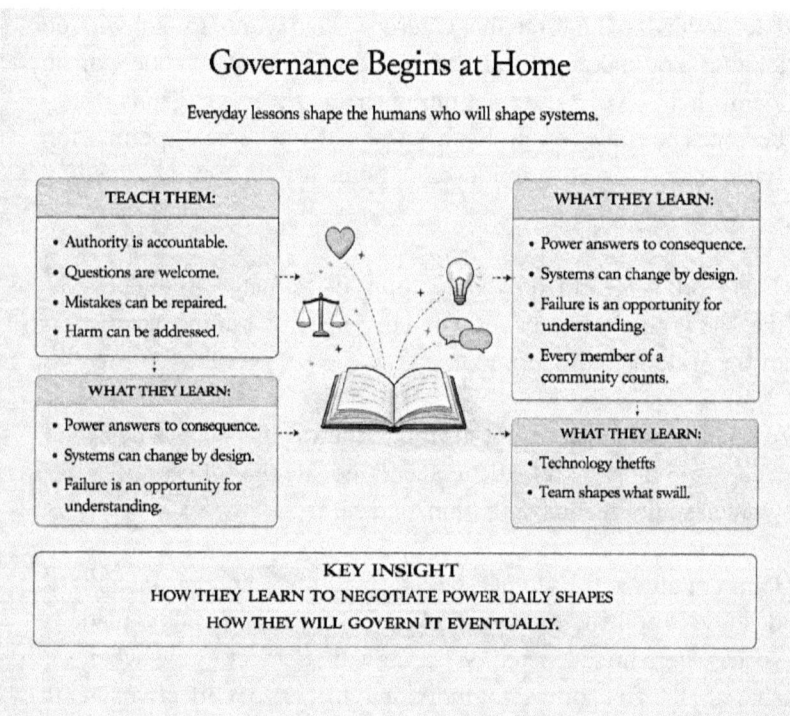

Governance Begins at Home

Everyday lessons shape the humans who will shape systems.

TEACH THEM:
- Authority is accountable.
- Questions are welcome.
- Mistakes can be repaired.
- Harm can be addressed.

WHAT THEY LEARN:
- Power answers to consequence.
- Systems can change by design.
- Failure is an opportunity for understanding.

WHAT THEY LEARN:
- Power answers to consequence.
- Systems can change by design.
- Failure is an opportunity for understanding.
- Every member of a community counts.

WHAT THEY LEARN:
- Technology thefts
- Team shapes what swill.

KEY INSIGHT
HOW THEY LEARN TO NEGOTIATE POWER DAILY SHAPES
HOW THEY WILL GOVERN IT EVENTUALLY.

GLOSSARY

Accountability: The obligation to answer for decisions and outcomes, including the capacity to intervene, repair, and redesign when harm occurs. Accountability without authority produces burnout; authority without accountability produces abuse.

Amygdala: A brain structure involved in threat detection and rapid emotional response. When highly activated, it can override reflective reasoning, prioritizing speed and defense over judgment.

Authorship: The power to define intent, values, boundaries, and acceptable risk within a system. Distinct from participation or contribution; authorship determines direction and consequence.

Authority: The legitimate power to make decisions, set priorities, and shape outcomes. In this book, authority is inseparable from responsibility for consequence.

Authority–Consequence Misalignment Pattern: The structural condition in which those who hold decision-making authority are insulated from the consequences of their decisions, while those closest to consequence are excluded from authority. This separation produces brittleness, erodes trust, and displaces responsibility onto those least positioned to address its source. It is the central pattern traced throughout this book.

Bias (Systems Bias): Structural distortion that emerges when pattern recognition is trained on incomplete histories, uneven power, or narrow success metrics. Bias is not a personal flaw but a systems property.

Care (as Systems Intelligence): The capacity to attend to relationship, context, and consequence over time. Care is diagnostic, anticipatory, and essential to system resilience, not an emotional accessory.

Continuity: The ability of systems to endure across time, context, and change without eroding trust, legitimacy, or coherence. Continuity is a core measure of intelligent governance.

Design Failure: A failure arising not from misuse or error, but from structural choices that separate authority from responsibility or ignore downstream consequence.

Differential Credibility: The systematic variation in how authority and expertise are recognized based on identity markers; manifests as gender bias where women's technical contributions face higher scrutiny and receive less automatic legitimacy.

Emotional Regulation: The capacity to integrate emotional signals with reflective reasoning, enabling judgment under pressure. Distinct from emotional suppression or reactivity.

Extraction: A design logic that prioritizes short-term gain, scale, and efficiency while externalizing cost, consequence, and depletion.

Feedback Loop: A process by which system outputs influence future inputs, reinforcing patterns over time. In biased systems, feedback loops compound inequality.

Gender Gap: Measurable disparities in representation, opportunity, compensation, or access between men and women; in technology contexts, includes leadership gaps (91–92% male executives), economic gaps (projected 123 years to close), and digital access gaps (15% lower mobile internet usage).

Gendered Architecture (of Authority): The structural arrangement of power that channels women toward responsibility for consequences while restricting their access to design authority and strategic decision-making.

Governance: The structures and practices through which authority, accountability, and responsibility are aligned. Governance is not an external constraint but an internal design feature.

Intelligence (Relational): The capacity to understand how information moves through living systems, including context, power, history, and consequence, not merely data processing or optimization.

Legitimacy: The belief that a system's authority is justified, accountable, and responsive to those it affects. Legitimacy cannot be declared; it must be earned and maintained.

Paternalism: A mode of authority that frames control as protection, guidance, or expertise while denying authorship to those expected to bear consequence.

Pattern Recognition: The core function of both human and artificial intelligence: identifying regularities and predicting outcomes based on prior data and assumptions.

Prefrontal Cortex: A brain region associated with reflective reasoning, impulse control, planning, and judgment. Central to emotional regulation and responsible decision-making.

Repair (Institutional): Efforts to stabilize systems after harm occurs, often through mediation or communication rather than redesign. Repair without authority delays failure but does not prevent it.

Responsibility: Obligation for consequence, often displaced downstream in large systems. Responsibility without authority is structurally unsustainable.

Sovereignty: The condition of operating from internal authority rather than waiting for external permission. In this book, sovereignty is not a legal or political term but a personal and structural one: the practice of claiming authorship, exercising power without apology, and refusing roles that absorb consequence without granting influence over design. Sovereignty is alignment, not arrogance.

Stewardship: A governance logic that prioritizes continuity, care, and responsibility for impact over time. Stewardship governs growth rather than surrendering to it.

Systems Intelligence: The capacity to perceive, anticipate, and respond to how systems behave over time, including unintended consequences and cumulative effects.

Trust: A judgment about whether a system or institution acts competently, fairly, and with accountability. Trust erodes when authority is distant from consequence.

REFERENCES

Boston Consulting Group. *The Gender Gap in Generative AI Adoption.* 2024.

Damasio, Antonio. *Descartes' Error: Emotion, Reason, and the Human Brain.* New York: G. P. Putnam's Sons, 1994.

Deloitte. *State of AI in the Enterprise Report.* 2023.

Eubanks, Virginia. *Automating Inequality: How High-Tech Tools Profile, Police, and Punish the Poor.* New York: St. Martin's Press, 2018.

Huang, Ziad Obermeyer, et al. "Dissecting Racial Bias in an Algorithm Used to Manage the Health of Populations." *Science* 366, no. 6464 (2019).

Noble, Safiya Umoja. *Algorithms of Oppression: How Search Engines Reinforce Racism.* New York: New York University Press, 2018.

O'Neil, Cathy. *Weapons of Math Destruction: How Big Data Increases Inequality and Threatens Democracy.* New York: Crown, 2016.

ProPublica. "Machine Bias." 2016.

Skillsoft. *Women in Tech Report.* 2024.

WomenTech Network. *Global Gender Gap and Women in Technology Report.* 2026 Assessment.

World Economic Forum. *Global Gender Gap Report.* 2023.

INDEX

Extraction: technology logic; labor; depletion; contrast with stewardship

Gender Diversity: business outcomes; McKinsey research; innovation benefits

Gender Gap: technology leadership; economic closure timeline; mobile internet access

Gendered Architecture: authority structures; responsibility without power; design exclusion

Governance: embedded vs. external; AI systems; legitimacy

Legitimacy: trust erosion; institutional failure; AI acceleration

Paternalism: authority without authorship; gendered systems
Responsibility: displacement; downstream burden; scale effects

Stewardship: authority requirement; system resilience; future design

Trust: asymmetry; burden of repair; system belief

Women in Technology: authorship loss; responsibility without authority; systems intelligence

ABOUT THE AUTHOR

Tadia Rice builds frameworks for governing intelligence.

She works at the intersection of technology, institutional design, and authority, examining how responsibility migrates through systems as decision-making disperses across networks of people and intelligent technologies.

Rice translates structural complexity into operational clarity. She converts abstract challenges, governance, ethics, technological power, into deployable structures for leaders accountable for scale.

Her central inquiry is architectural: how authority is designed, how accountability fragments, and why intelligence without stewardship produces fragility rather than resilience.

She treats ethics not as restraint, but as infrastructure, necessary for systems that intend to endure.

Her books explore technology and human agency in an era of accelerating intelligence:
Governing Intelligence: A Guide for Responsible Leadership
AI, Unity, and the Emerging Human Future
The AI Arms Race: Power, Competition, and Who Controls Intelligence
Artificial Intelligence & Human Consciousness: Crossing the Threshold
Growing Up With Intelligence: How AI Is Shaping Generations
My Conversations with AI: 100 Questions

This body of work examines systems sustained by invisible labor, displaced responsibility, and informal governance, and what fractures when those dynamics scale beyond accountability.

Rice's advisory work draws from direct experience inside institutions where technological capacity advanced faster than governance structures. She has guided public institutions, mission-driven organizations, and cross-sector leaders navigating intelligence, power, and public trust.

Inside the System, Outside the Power names a structural condition: participation without authorship. Operating within a system while remaining unable to shape its design. The condition intensifies as authority becomes automated and decision-making grows opaque.

Rice frames the challenge directly:
Who authors the intelligence we create?
And who bears its consequences?

Her work insists that durable systems require alignment between authority and responsibility. Without that alignment, intelligence scales. Legitimacy does not.